AFTER

T·H·E

CRASH

AFTER

T·H·E

CRASH

LINKAGES BETWEEN STOCKS & FUTURES

William J. Brodsky
John C. Coffee, Jr.
Joel J. Cohen
Thomas Coleman
Robert Davis
Franklin Edwards
Joseph Grundfest
Philip McBride Johnson
Thomas Eric Kilcollin
Roger M. Kubarych
Merton H. Miller
Hans R. Stoll
Paula Tosini
Richard Zecher
Robert J. Mackay, editor

American Enterprise
Institute for Public
Policy Research
Washington, D.C.

Distributed by arrangement with
UPA, Inc.

4720 Boston Way   3 Henrietta Street
Lanham, Md. 20706   London WC2E 8LU England

LIBRARY OF CONGRESS
Library of Congress Cataloging-in-Publication Data

After the crash : linkages between stocks and futures/Robert J.
  Mackay, ed.; William J. Brodsky . . . [et al.].
        p.   cm. — (AEI studies ; 477)
    ISBN 0-8447-3663-5 (pbk. : alk. paper)
    1. Stocks—United States. 2. Stock-index futures—United States.
    3. Stock-exchange—United States. I. Mackay, Robert J.
    II. Brodsky, William J. III. Series.
    HG4910.A64 1988   88-14605
    332.63'222—dc 19   CIP

1 3 5 7 9 10 8 6 4 2

AEI Studies 477

Contents

Contributors

WILLIAM J. BRODSKY is the president and chief executive officer of the Chicago Mercantile Exchange. Before joining the CME, he worked with the American Stock Exchange and with the New York investment banking and securities brokerage firm of Model, Roland and Company. Mr. Brodsky received an A.B. degree from Syracuse University and a J.D. degree from the Syracuse University College of Law.

JOHN C. COFFEE, JR., is the Adolf A. Berle Professor of Law at Columbia University Law School, specializing in corporate law. Before teaching at several law schools, including Stanford University, the University of Virginia, the University of Michigan, and Georgetown University, Mr. Coffee practiced law as an associate with the New York firm of Cravath Swaine & Moore. Mr. Coffee received his education at Amherst College, Yale University, where he received his LL.B., and New York University, where he received his LL.M. in taxation.

JOEL J. COHEN served as general counsel for the Presidential Task Force on Market Mechanisms (the Brady commission). He was formerly a partner with the New York law firm of Davis Polk & Wardwell, where he practiced corporate law. Mr. Cohen received his B.B.A. from the City College of New York and a J.D. degree from Harvard Law School.

THOMAS COLEMAN is vice president and director of economic analysis and planning for the Chicago Board of Trade, where he supervised the development of financial futures and options-on-futures contracts created since 1987. Mr. Coleman received his bachelor's and master's degrees from the University of Chicago, where he also did doctoral work.

ROBERT DAVIS has been commissioner of the Commodity Futures Trading Commission since October 1984 and serves as chairman of the CFTC Financial Products Advisory Committee. Before joining the commission, he served as senior economist for the Joint Economic Committee of the United States Congress and was on the economics faculty at Vanderbilt University. Mr. Davis attended Virginia Polytechnic Institute, where he received B.A., M.A., and Ph.D. degrees in economics.

FRANKLIN EDWARDS is a professor in the Graduate School of Business and director of the Center for the Study of Futures Markets at Columbia University. He holds a Ph.D. from Harvard University and a J.D. degree from New York University.

JOSEPH GRUNDFEST has been a commissioner of the Securities and Exchange Commission since October 1985. He has also served as counsel and senior economist for legal and regulatory matters at the President's Council of Economic Advisers and practiced law with Wilmer, Cutler & Pickering. He was an economist with the Rand Corporation and the Brookings Institution. Mr. Grundfest was educated at Yale University, the London School of Economics, and Stanford University.

PHILIP MCBRIDE JOHNSON is a partner in the New York–based law firm of Skadden, Arps, Slate, Meagher & Flom. From 1981 to 1983, he served as chairman of the Commodity Futures Trading Commission. Mr. Johnson received his LL.B. degree from Yale University.

THOMAS ERIC KILCOLLIN has been executive vice president and chief economist with the Chicago Mercantile Exchange since August 1987. He served as an economist at the Board of Governors of the Federal Reserve System from 1978 to 1981. Mr. Kilcollin received his bachelor's degree from Georgetown University and Ph.D. in economics from the University of Chicago.

ROGER M. KUBARYCH has been senior vice president and chief economist at the New York Stock Exchange since April 1986. From 1971 to 1985 Mr. Kubarych held various positions at the Federal Reserve Bank of New York and the United States Treasury. He has an M.A. in economics from Harvard University and has completed coursework there for a Ph.D. in economics.

ROBERT J. MACKAY is professor of economics and associate director of the graduate economics program at Virginia Polytechnic Institute and State University (Virginia Tech) in northern Virginia. He was project director for the Commodity Futures Trading Commission's Financial

Products Advisory Committee's study of the hedging definition and the use of financial futures and options. Mr. Mackay received his Ph.D. in economics from the University of North Carolina.

MERTON H. MILLER is the Robert R. McCormick Distinguished Service Professor of Finance at the Graduate School of Business, University of Chicago. He has served at the U.S. Treasury and with the Board of Governors of the Federal Reserve System, and was an assistant lecturer at the London School of Economics. Mr. Miller received his A.B. from Harvard University and his Ph.D. from Johns Hopkins University.

HANS R. STOLL is the Anne Marie and Thomas B. Walker, Jr., Professor of Finance at the Owen Graduate School of Management at Vanderbilt University, where he serves as the director of the Ph.D. program in management. He also taught at the Wharton School at the University of Pennsylvania and the University of Chicago and served with the Securities and Exchange Commission on the Institutional Investor Study. Mr. Stoll has a Ph.D. from the University of Chicago.

PAULA TOSINI is chief economist and director of the Division of Economic Analysis for the Commodity Futures Trading Commission, where she had served as director of research. Earlier she served as legislative assistant to Senator Richard Lugar. Ms. Tosini received a B.S. degree in foreign service from Georgetown University, a certificate from the University of Brussels, an M.S. in foreign service from Georgetown University, and a Ph.D. in economics from the University of Maryland, where she is a lecturer in the College of Business and Management.

RICHARD ZECHER is treasurer and senior vice president of the Chase Manhattan Bank. He joined the Chase Manhattan Corporation in 1981 as chief economist and assumed his current responsibilities in 1986. He was previously a senior economist with the U.S. Council of Economic Advisers, director of economics and policy research for the Securities and Exchange Commission and dean of the Iowa College of Business Administration. Mr. Zecher received his M.B.A. in economics from the University of Delaware and his Ph.D. from Ohio State University.

Introduction

Robert J. Mackay

On October 19, 1987, one of the longest and most spectacular bull markets in U.S. stock market history came to a definitive and dramatic end. The Dow Jones Industrial Average fell 508 points, or 22.6 percent, in the largest one-day drop in history. The decline on Black Monday, as October 19 has come to be known, rivaled the two-day drop on October 28 and 29, 1929, of 24.5 percent. Black Monday came on the heels of three onerous trading days in which the Dow fell a total of 261 points, or roughly 10 percent. In the four trading days ending on October 19, the value of U.S. stocks dropped more than 30 percent, or nearly $1 trillion.

Trading on October 20, the day after Black Monday, was marked by extreme price volatility. Stock and stock index futures prices were up sharply at the open with a temporary rally, then fluctuated within a 450-point range throughout the day, and closed with a gain of 108 points. The rally continued on Wednesday, but the gains did not last long. By Monday, October 26, the Dow stood at 1793, just 55 points over its close on Black Monday.

Since the beginning of the bull market five years earlier, the Dow went from a low of 776 in August 1982 to a peak of 2722 in August 1987. By the end of 1987, after the dust from the crash had finally settled, the Dow stood at about the same level it had just one year earlier.

Market-making capacity was severely strained during the crash. The volume of shares traded on the New York Stock Exchange (NYSE) set back-to-back records on October 19 and 20, topping 600 million shares each day. On October 19, during the first hour of trading alone, nearly 100 million shares were traded. This unusually large volume was coupled with large order imbalances for individual stocks. On October 19 there were 195 trading delays and halts lasting an average of 51 minutes for Standard and Poor (S&P) 500 stocks; on October 20 there were 280 trading delays and halts, averaging 78 minutes. System backlogs caused many trades to be delayed or to go unexecuted.

Traders had difficulty determining when, or even if, their trades had been executed and at what price.

Linkages between the stock market and the stock index futures markets were also strained. On Monday, October 19, the S&P 500 futures contract opened at an unusually large discount to the reported value of the index, a discount of roughly 19 points or 7 percent. A large apparent discount persisted throughout much of the day. Because of the disorderly conditions in the cash market, arbitrage traders found it difficult to execute index arbitrage and, as a result, reduced their activity. On October 20 so many stocks were not trading that the Chicago Board Options Exchange temporarily suspended trading in its index options. The Chicago Mercantile Exchange followed suit with a temporary suspension of trading in the S&P 500 futures.

The crash was by no means limited to U.S. markets; indeed, it was worldwide. Although the performance of stock markets typically varies widely across countries, stock prices in all major countries of the world fell in October. Declines were generally in excess of 20 percent.[1] Moreover, major declines abroad preceded the U.S. decline on October 19. The stock markets in Hong Kong, Malaysia, and Singapore all declined in the twelve to twenty-four hours before October 19. A number of European countries experienced large declines on October 19, which (because North American markets are the last to trade) also preceded the U.S. decline. Although most markets rallied on October 21, many suffered marked declines for the rest of October. October losses amounted to 45.8 percent in Hong Kong, 22.1 percent in the United Kingdom, and 41.6 percent in Singapore, as compared with 21.6 percent in the United States.

Studies of the Crash

The crash has left many people, both in and out of government, wondering what happened, why it happened, and what, if anything, can be done to prevent it from happening again. Within four months of the crash, several studies had been completed and submitted to various exchanges, government agencies, congressional committees, and the president in an attempt to answer these questions. The first report was the interim report of the Commodity Futures Trading Commission (CFTC) released on November 9, 1987. The CFTC released a follow-up report on January 6, 1988.

The stock and futures exchanges followed with a pair of reports in late December. Nicholas deB. Katzenbach, who had been commissioned before the crash by the New York Stock Exchange to study program trading, submitted his report (the Katzenbach report) on December 21, 1987. This report addressed the role of futures-related trading in the crash. The Chicago Mercantile Exchange appointed a committee composed of Merton Miller (chairman), John Hawke, Jr., Burton Malkiel, and Myron Scholes to study the role of stock index futures in the crash. The committee's report (the CME report) was submitted on December 22, 1987.

The Presidential Task Force, appointed by President Reagan in October and chaired by former senator Nicholas Brady, submitted its much-anticipated study on January 8, 1988, to the president, the secretary of the Treasury, and the chairman of the Federal Reserve Board. The so-called Brady commission report has become the most prominent and certainly the most widely cited of all the reports.

On January 26, 1988, the General Accounting Office submitted its report (the GAO report) to various members of Congress. This was followed on January 29 by the release of the CFTC's final report. This first round of studies was completed in February when the Securities and Exchange Commission released its study, the SEC report. Complete citations for all of these studies can be found in the Appendix on page 85 of this book.

Taken together, the studies provide a wealth of information on the crash. They paint a detailed picture (or, more accurately, set of pictures) of the events surrounding October 19, especially those on the eight trading days from October 14 through October 23. Although the studies reach different and sometimes contradictory conclusions about the underlying cause of the crash and the factors that contributed to its speed and severity, they have one important factor in common: each focuses on the role of derivative markets for stock index futures and options.

The Brady report, for example, concludes that futures-related trading, including portfolio insurance and index arbitrage, played a key role in the crash. According to the Brady report:

> The precipitous market decline of October was "triggered" by specific events: an unexpectedly high merchandise trade deficit which pushed interest rates to new high levels, and proposed tax legislation which led to the collapse of the stocks of a number of takeover candidates. This initial decline ignited mechanical, price-insensitive selling by a number of institutions following portfolio insurance strategies and a small number of mutual fund groups. The selling by these investors, and the prospect for further selling by them, encouraged a number of aggressive trading-oriented

3

institutions to sell in anticipation of further declines . . . .This selling in turn stimulated further reactive
selling by portfolio insurers and mutual funds.
Portfolio insurers sold in both the stock market and the
stock index futures market. Selling pressure in the futures
market was transmitted to the stock market by the mechanism of index arbitrage. (p. v)

The CFTC final report, in contrast, points to a fundamental
realignment of investor perceptions about the value of stocks, as
opposed to trading in stock index futures. According to the CFTC
report:

The wave of selling that engulfed the global securities markets on October 19 was not initiated by trading in index
products nor did it principally emanate from such trading.
There was a massive change in investor perceptions, building from the previous week's experience, about the value of
stocks, and many investors acted simultaneously and in
unprecedented volumes upon those changed perceptions.
(p. 81)
In sum, the analysis of intra-day trading does not support a contention that on October 19 the stock market fell as
fast and as far as it did because of a continuously intensifying
interaction between index arbitrage stock sales and portfolio
insurance selling in the futures markets. (pp. 95–96)

The SEC report, going beyond the Brady commission's report in
its indictment of futures-related trading, and contrasting with the
CFTC final report, concludes that:

Futures trading and strategies involving the use of futures
were not the "sole cause" of the market break. Nevertheless,
the existence of futures on stock indexes and use of the
various strategies involving "program trading" were a significant factor in accelerating and exacerbating the declines.
(p. xiii)
Three dramatic trends have occurred as a result of trading in derivative index products. First, stock index futures
have supplemented and often replaced the secondary stock
market as the primary price discovery mechanism for stocks.
Second, the availability of the futures market has spawned
institutional trading strategies that have greatly increased
the velocity and concentration of stock trading. Third, the
resulting increase in index arbitrage and portfolio insurance
trading in the stock market has increased the risks incurred

4

by stock specialists and has strained and at times exceeded their ability to provide liquidity to the stock market. (p. xiv)

The focus on the role of stock index futures, so clearly evident in these quotes, can be appreciated in light of market developments before the crash. Most notably, institutional investors—major users of these products—had grown very rapidly. At the time of the crash, pension funds, mutual funds, life insurance companies, endowments, and broker-dealers commanded a major share of the U.S. equity market in relation to both the value of stocks held and trading volume. The growth of institutional investors, coupled with the rapid growth of index funds and funds managed under portfolio insurance schemes, created a tremendous demand for trading baskets or entire portfolios of stocks, known as program trading. The stock index futures contract provided a means of satisfying this demand. Because of its liquidity and low transactions costs, the futures market became the "market of choice" for institutional investors actively trading in the market. Between 1982 and 1987 the daily volume of trading in stock index futures grew to more than twice the average daily dollar volume of trading on the NYSE.

Futures were the "new kid" on the financial block, and they were attracting a lot of attention. Before the crash, in 1986, attention focused on the effect of stock index futures on stock price volatility on expiration Fridays. At the time, there were four days each year when stock index futures, options on stock index futures, and stock index options all expired simultaneously at the close. The unwinding of index arbitrage programs created large order imbalances and price volatility in the final hour of trading, which came to be known as the "triple witching hour." The problem appeared to be solved when expirations were moved to the opening, but concern about an apparent connection between index arbitrage and stock price volatility remained. More attention was focused on the issue in the months just before the crash when John Phelan, chairman of the NYSE, began expressing concern about a "market meltdown." His now famous "cascade scenario" was premised on a view of how index arbitrage and portfolio insurance might interact adversely.

Another reason why futures became a focus of the reports is that there were large apparent discounts in the futures market when trading began on October 19. Unprecedented discounts in the S&P 500 futures contract, for example, seemed to suggest that the crash started in the futures markets in Chicago and that it was transmitted to the cash markets in New York through index arbitrage.

The Issues

The events of October and the studies that followed have raised important questions about the functioning of our financial markets. The sharpness and size of the price break have raised the issue of whether preplanned circuit breakers—across-the-board trading pauses and price limits—might provide a more orderly adjustment than the present system of ad hoc circuit breakers, which is implicit in delayed openings and individual trading halts based on order imbalances. The crash itself has raised concern about excessive speculation. Some are concerned that excessive speculation, fueled by excessive leverage in the futures market, created a speculative bubble that made the crash all but inevitable. These concerns have led to calls for increased margins in the futures markets.

The potential for financial collapse on October 20, given the rumored insolvency of some key participants, has led market analysts and regulators to take a closer look at clearing, payment, and credit systems. The huge intermarket transfers of funds required during the week of October 19 have led to a search by some for ways to reduce liquidity demands. This search has resulted in proposals for sharing information across exchanges on pays and collects regarding variation margin, proposals for cross margining between futures, options, and cash positions on different exchanges, and proposals for a unified clearing system. Even the basic market-making systems have been questioned. The specialist system has been criticized as inappropriate for trading baskets of stocks, and the open outcry system used in the futures pit has been criticized as contributing to price volatility.

Finally, questions have been raised about the proper regulatory structure for interrelated cash, futures, and options markets. In light of the different views about the factors contributing to the crash, it is not surprising that some conflicting policy recommendations have been put forward. The Katzenbach report, for example, recommends giving the Securities and Exchange Commission regulatory authority over all financial futures. The Brady commission report recommends that a single agency, preferably the Federal Reserve Board, be given authority over critical intermarket regulatory issues. The chairman of the SEC, David Ruder, has called instead for shifting regulatory jurisdiction. He proposes shifting from the CFTC to the SEC the authority to regulate all stock index products, including stock index futures, options on stock index futures, and options on stock indexes. The chairman of the CFTC, Wendy Gramm, opposes both the Brady proposal and the Ruder proposal. Finally, the GAO report calls on the existing cast of regulators to develop integrated, intermarket contingency plans.

After the Crash

The important process of sorting through these studies, evaluating their disparate diagnoses, and weighing their recommendations for reform has just begun. On February 24, 1988, at its headquarters in Washington, the American Enterprise Institute held a policy forum organized by Marvin Kosters, director of economic policy studies at AEI. The forum, "After the Crash: The Financial Markets Studies and Policy Proposals," was the first major step in this process. Regulators, knowledgeable market participants, and leading academic experts—many of whom were involved in the preparation of these studies—were brought together to discuss their views of what happened, why it happened, what the regulatory response should be, and how financial and market-making systems should be restructured. This volume is based on the proceedings of AEI's forum.

This volume is divided into four parts. Part One deals with the causes of the crash and the implications for public policy. Joel J. Cohen, general counsel to the Brady commission; Merton H. Miller, professor of finance at the University of Chicago and coauthor of the CME report; Joseph Grundfest, commissioner of the SEC; Robert Davis, commissioner of the CFTC; and Franklin Edwards, professor and director of the Columbia University Futures Center, present their views.

Part Two deals with regulatory issues involving the setting of margins on futures and stocks and the appropriateness of circuit breakers such as price limits and trading halts. This section offers the views of Hans Stoll, professor of finance and director of the Financial Markets Research Center at Vanderbilt University; Thomas Coleman, vice president and director of economic analysis at the Chicago Board of Trade; Paula Tosini, director of the Division of Economic Analysis at the CFTC; and Richard Zecher, treasurer and senior vice president of the Chase Manhattan Bank.

Part Three is a statement by William J. Brodsky, president and chief executive officer of the Chicago Mercantile Exchange, of how the Chicago Merc is responding to the crash and the recommendations in the Brady report regarding clearing and settlement procedures, information flows, margin requirements, financial safeguards, and circuit breakers.

Part Four deals with the advantages and disadvantages of alternative market-making systems; the need for modifications in clearing, credit, and payment systems; and the role of large institutional investors in the crash. The views of John C. Coffee, Jr., professor at Columbia University; Philip McBride Johnson, partner at Skadden,

Arps, Slate, Meagher & Flom and former chairman of the CFTC;
Thomas Eric Kilcollin, senior vice president and chief economist at the
Chicago Mercantile Exchange; and Roger Kubarych, senior vice president and chief economist at the New York Stock Exchange are presented in this section. In this volume we have drawn together some of
the most informed thinking on these crucial public policy issues. We
hope that it will help put these studies of the crash and their recommendations into proper perspective.

Note

1. Information on the international scope of the crash is presented in
Richard Roll, "The International Crash of October 1987," (unpublished working paper, UCLA, April 1988).

PART ONE

Explaining the Events of October 1987

Joel J. Cohen

General Counsel
Brady Task Force

To put the recommendations of the Brady task force in perspective, I want to address the particular events that gave rise to them. The market break in October 1987 started on the thirteenth of that month. In the four trading days between October 13 and October 19, the value of all outstanding stocks in the United States dropped by about a trillion dollars. What quickly became apparent to the task force was that notwithstanding the enormous volumes of shares and futures contracts traded, only 3 percent of the publicly held stock changed hands during those four trading days. Yet this 3 percent resulted in the loss of one trillion dollars in value. To us this revealed an unusual frailty in the market, which we decided to study in depth.

In the very short time that we had available to conduct our study, we wanted to learn as much as possible about who was buying and who was selling during those four trading days. What we determined was that there were three categories of major players. The first category involved institutional traders following reactive strategies. These institutions included portfolio insurers as well as mutual funds that faced enormous redemptions beginning on Friday, October 16.

The second category included what we referred to as "aggressive trading-oriented institutions." In addition to hedge funds, these were a small number of pension and endowment funds, money management firms, and investment banking firms that knew the basic strategies that the portfolio insurers were following, knew what the computer models were directing the portfolio insurers to do, and knew that the mutual funds were facing large redemptions. These institutions anticipated the massive selling of investors following these reactive strategies and sold with the ultimate goal of repurchasing at lower prices.

The third category included the index arbitrageurs, traders who attempt to profit from price disparities between the futures market and the stock market.

11

During the three trading days preceding October 19, portfolio insurers sold massive amounts of futures: about $500 million worth of futures contracts on Wednesday, which was about 14 percent of the public volume; about $965 million worth on Thursday, which was almost 20 percent of the public volume; and $2.1 billion worth on Friday, which was about 26 percent of the public volume. But, according to their computer models, portfolio insurers were still far behind by the close on Friday. From our analysis it appeared that there was an overhang going into Monday of portfolio insurance sales yet to be executed of about $8 billion. Portfolio insurers sold almost $2 billion worth of stock and about $4 billion worth of futures contracts on Monday, October 19. That compares with a total of about $21 billion in stock market transactions and $20 billion in futures market transactions that day.

Mutual funds, it appeared, had about $750 million in excess redemptions over sales by Friday. All of these transactions had to be executed by Monday, because the mutual funds had promised to give value for shares redeemed based on the closing price on Friday. A few mutual funds sold almost a billion dollars worth of stock on Monday.

In the stock market, the top fifteen sellers on October 19 accounted for 20 percent of the total sales, or $4 billion. The top fifteen buyers accounted for 10 percent of the volume, or $2 billion. Index arbitrage involved about $1.7 billion worth of stock.

In the futures market, the concentration of trading among big players was even more significant. Portfolio insurers sold $4 billion worth of stock index futures contracts, which was about 40 percent of the public volume. The top ten sellers accounted for 50 percent of the volume.

The result was that all the markets were virtually overwhelmed with massive, one-sided volume. Specialists could not cope. The New York Stock Exchange automated systems could not cope. The over-the-counter markets did not cope well; their communication lines were jammed, and their automated execution systems did not work. The futures market plummeted as well. There was just not enough capital or enough buy-side interest. The Dow Jones Industrial Index (Dow) closed down a record 508 points.

In our view, Tuesday, October 20, was the worst day for the financial markets. The entire financial system looked as if it were about to collapse by midday on Tuesday. The serious problems began at about 11 a.m., when the sell-side volume started to overwhelm the market makers. There was virtually no market-making ability left after Monday. Certainly the specialists on the New York Stock Exchange had gone home Monday night with very large inventories of stocks.

On top of this, rumors started circulating in the Wall Street community, and in Chicago as well, that certain of the Chicago clearinghouses would have serious problems meeting their obligations to their clearing members. The rumors turned out not to be true. In fact, though, two major investment banking firms were owed variation margin payments of about $1.5 billion from the Chicago Mercantile Exchange clearinghouse. Ordinarily such margin would have been paid first thing in the morning, but it was not paid until five or six hours later. The enormous demands for liquidity due to the variation margin calls were causing problems for the major market participants.

We did not find tangible evidence that the banks actually pulled credit lines during this critical period; but most of the credit arrangements between market participants and banks are based on uncommitted credit. There are virtually no committed credit lines. Market participants rely on the money's being available when it is needed. We did find, however, that a number of the major banks, while not cutting off credit, apparently slowed the credit approval process significantly, and we heard that a number of foreign banks discontinued lending to the Wall Street community.

Certainly, it helped a great deal when the Federal Reserve announced on Tuesday that it would increase liquidity to the market. But by then things had come close to gridlock. Tuesday, then, was the day that concerned us the most. Trading in many stocks halted at about noon on Tuesday; the Chicago Mercantile Exchange closed for an hour and a half because it thought that the New York Stock Exchange would close; the Chicago Board Options Exchange stayed virtually closed all day because it had so many options in rotation; and many people were having trouble getting liquidity to fund the obligations that they had.

The problems on Monday and Tuesday seemed to have been exacerbated by unprecedented discounts between the futures market and the stock market, which ordinarily would prompt index arbitrage. That did not happen for two reasons. Arbitrageurs rely on the New York Stock Exchange's designated-order turnaround (DOT) system, the automated order execution system. This system is the quickest and cheapest way to execute large orders involving the sale or purchase of baskets of stocks. The DOT system broke down on Monday afternoon because the massive volume overwhelmed the system. Orders got so backed up, and order execution was so unreliable, that arbitrageurs did not know when their orders were going to be executed or at what prices their orders had been executed. Arbitrage under those circumstances was impossible and virtually dried up by 2 p.m. on Monday.

On Tuesday arbitrage was further limited because the New York Stock Exchange announced that member firms could not use the DOT system for index arbitrage. This made a lot of sense from the point of view of the New York Stock Exchange but probably not from the point of view of the overall financial system and the linking of the two markets. There were enormous discounts in the futures market, which persisted because of the absence of arbitrage. Persistent discounts of this magnitude were unprecedented. People looked at the futures market and saw it forecasting a much lower level for the Dow. The futures market at one point was down to a Dow equivalent of about 1300 rather than just 1700. These discounts discouraged people from buying stocks. As a result, both the stock market and the futures market went into a virtual free fall.

The delinking of these two markets appeared to us to be a major problem. It may explain why all the markets declined so rapidly during those two days. This led the task force to what we considered a fairly obvious conclusion: the futures market, the options market, and the stock market are really a single market. The instruments are fundamentally driven by the same economic forces; the same financial institutions are the major players in all these markets; trading strategies such as portfolio insurance and index arbitrage link these markets, as do clearing and settlement procedures.

In recognition of these important links, we concluded that the regulation of the stock, futures, and options markets should be better organized. A single agency should be charged with the responsibility for regulating certain important intermarket issues. At present, the Securities and Exchange Commission (SEC) regulates the stock market and the options market, while the Commodity Futures Trading Commission (CFTC) regulates the futures market. No one agency looks across all these markets and makes sure that they work in harmony.

The task force did not envision adding a whole new layer of regulation. Adequate regulation already exists. We simply suggested that the regulation be organized and coordinated in a more rational manner. From our analysis, we selected four issues that raised significant intermarket concerns. First, and probably the most important, is the unification of the credit and clearing mechanisms. The fragmentation of the different clearinghouses, coupled with the massive volume and violent price movements, created an enormous demand for liquidity on Monday and Tuesday. This, in turn, resulted in tremendous flows of funds through the banking system, which the clearing and banking system had difficulty coping with.

The Federal Reserve wire went down at certain points, which was a very serious problem, and no one was sure that it would stay open late enough on Monday night to ensure that everyone got paid. There ought to be a better way to organize the mechanics of clearing.

We look upon this as a mechanical problem. It was never a solvency problem. There were rumors of insolvency, of course, which turned out to be unfounded. But because participants believed that there was nobody monitoring the intermarket exposure of firms that operate across these markets, these rumors created a lot of uncertainty.

The task force does not particularly care whether there is one clearinghouse or several clearinghouses. The point is that they should be organized and unified in some manner. Someone needs to look across market exposures. This would also help liquidity. Banks would be in a better position to make credit decisions if they knew the overall financial position of people operating in different markets, not just their futures position or their stock position.

The second issue, which I need not comment further on here, is the margin issue. The task force believed that margin requirements ought to be harmonized between the stock and the futures markets.

The third issue is information. Simply put, there is a tremendous amount of information about who is buying and selling in the futures market. The same type of information, large-trader data, is not available for the stock market. This made it very difficult for us, and for others studying the events of October, to determine who was actually buying or selling. That information should be available.

The final issue is circuit breakers. Ad hoc circuit breakers now exist. The New York Stock Exchange decided to stop trading in stocks, because of order imbalances. The Chicago Mercantile Exchange decided to close down because it thought the New York Stock Exchange was closing down. The DOT system backed up, and access was limited so that index arbitrage was prevented. Each of these were circuit breakers, but they were not organized rationally.

We heard a lot of people say that they would have bought stock on Monday or Tuesday if they could only have had ten minutes to figure out what to buy and how to get their brokers on the phone. All the task force is recommending is that there be some coordinated time-out mechanism to allow people the ten minutes they need to think and to try to get organized. This might bring value buyers back

15

into the market at a time like October 19 or 20.

Who should be responsible for these intermarket issues? We considered a variety of committees and agencies, but it seemed logical to us that it should be the Federal Reserve. We leave that to other people to judge, however.

Merton H. Miller

University of Chicago

The Chicago Mercantile Exchange invited me and three others to look into the events of October 19 and especially to evaluate the role of stock index futures. We were not convened to bring a fresh new perspective to the role of futures—we had all written extensively about those markets in the past. All of us shared the view, which is virtually universal among academics in the field of finance, that index futures markets are not just gambling casinos but are important contributors to the liquidity and efficiency of the capital markets. If, however, the facts showed that futures markets were at fault in October, the Chicago Mercantile Exchange wanted to be the first to know it.

After looking at all the data compiled by the exchange staff, we came to four main conclusions about the role of futures.

First, the presence of an index futures market in the United States—at that time virtually only in the United States—cannot credibly be charged with the substantial worldwide rise in equity values between January and September 1987. Was it part of the picture? Clearly it was. But let us be sensible about this. At no time was the total open interest in futures much over 1 percent of the total value of equities outstanding. It is true that trading volume in futures is more than this; but that is because, as the joke has it, futures are trading sardines, not eating sardines. If we want to evaluate the impact of futures in terms of value, we have to look at the open interest.

Between January and September 1987 equity values in the United States rose 30 percent. This was roughly in the middle of the increases, worldwide over this period. Perhaps one percentage point of that increase might be attributable to the enhanced liquidity and the risk-shifting possibilities offered by futures. That the contribution might be as much as 3 percent is arguable, but 30 percent just cannot be attributed to futures.

Second, we showed that contrary to reports widely circulating at

17

the time and still being repeated in the press, the crash did not originate in Chicago and flow from there to an otherwise calm and unsuspecting New York market. The tidal wave of selling hit both markets simultaneously. The evidence is crystal clear on this point.

It only seemed to hit Chicago first, because so many of the stocks did not open on time in New York on Monday. As a result, the published index of stock prices was still reflecting the hopelessly out-of-date prices at the Friday close. This reporting lag explains a large part of the apparent discount between the futures market and the cash market. I think the record will show that no one made any money on arbitrage on that opening gap. The fall had already occurred in New York; it just was not being registered on the dials.

I was surprised to learn from Mr. Cohen's presentation that so many sophisticated people in New York were apparently unaware of how those numbers are put together and failed to realize that the futures index, under those conditions, had zero predictive power.

Third, the futures market, rather than transmitting selling pressure to New York by program trading—as has been charged—on balance absorbed net selling pressure by a substantial amount. We estimate the absorption at the equivalent of about 85 million shares that might otherwise have been sold on the New York Stock Exchange.

Finally, the futures markets were no more the source of the dramatic turnaround on Tuesday than they had been the source of the dive on Monday morning. The fresh infusions of buying power on October 20 from both corporate buy-backs and Federal Reserve sustained dealer positioning turned the tide. It was not a psychological lift coming from the major market index or from shutting down program trading on the New York Stock Exchange.

The Federal Reserve support for the market, which proved so critical, was by no means out of the ordinary. Basically the same thing was done in 1929. Central bankers know how to respond to threatened localized liquidity crises. That is their business. It is the subtler kind of crisis, as in 1931, that bankers have trouble handling.

If some sense a difference, at least in tone, between our report and some of the subsequent ones, it may simply reflect the feelings of some members of our panel that portfolio insurance was getting far too much attention. Certainly substantial portfolio insurance selling did occur on October 19. Nobody denies that. But the fall in stock prices on that day was more than a matter of the actions of a few big price-insensitive sellers, as the Brady report often seems to suggest. There was also substantial selling by others. In fact, the value of selling by others on the New York Stock Exchange was three to five

18

times as large as the selling by portfolio insurers.

The ultimate absurdity in overstating the role of futures-related trading was surely provided by the SEC report. The staff of the SEC informs us that portfolio insurance and index arbitrage, though accounting for no more than 20 percent of the New York Stock Exchange volume during the entire day of October 19 and no more than 40 percent during the fateful hour between 1:00 and 2:00 P.M., nevertheless accounted for "more than 60 percent of the S&P stock volume at three 10-minute intervals within that hour." In fact, since trades are recorded sequentially, there must surely have been ten-second intervals in which portfolio insurance accounted for 100 percent of the trades. Such an observation provides virtually no meaningful information.

There is a way to get on the other side of the portfolio insurance strategy and take advantage of it. That is simply to adopt another strategy that many of us have already adopted, a constant proportion strategy—a strategy of always keeping, say, 50 percent of one's wealth in equities and 50 percent in fixed income. With this strategy one is in effect selling portfolio insurance. The SEC should look into the obstacles that keep people from being able to take that other kind of strategy and selling portfolio insurance.

Although our factual conclusions are not out of line with those of the Brady commission, we do part company when it comes to their four policy recommendations.

First, their call for a single overriding regulatory agency strikes me as the kind of recommendation that would be offered by a chief executive officer or a board chairman, like most of the people on the Brady task force, rather than by an academic, like those on our panel. Academics are more accustomed to collegial persuasion as a way of getting things done than to hierarchical decision making. The Federal Reserve has, quite wisely, backed away from that proposal.

Second, the call for a unified clearing system is reminiscent of the grand-sounding but impractical proposals offered fifteen years ago for a national market system. It strikes me and others on the panel as an overreaction to the rumors of clearing defaults that were floating, particularly in New York, during this chaotic period. We are aware of those rumors, but the first we heard about them was when we read about them in the Brady report. They were not a major factor on the floor of the Chicago Mercantile Exchange.

By ordinary standards the clearing process worked remarkably smoothly in Chicago, given the huge amounts of money involved. Of course, to outsiders clearinghouses always look as if they are on the brink. They are thinly capitalized enterprises that succeed by moving very fast. But they know their business, and they have met the acid test: they have survived. They have survived not only this shock but many earlier ones.

The clearing-related problems that were encountered in Chicago were mainly in the options market not in the futures market. The options markets are newer, and the calculations involved there are a bit trickier. This was their first real crash. They have learned some lessons. If they and there supporting banks—the Chicago banks were very supportive—ever get the chance, they will certainly do better next time.

Third, the recommendations regarding clearing are less serious than the ones about futures margins. The issue of futures margins and who sets them are more than just organizational details. There are delicate business trade-offs involved. In my view, taking these business decisions away from the private sector, where the incentives are right, and transferring them to the public sector, where the incentives are wrong, will ultimately kill the futures industry. Regulators never lose by setting margins high. In fact, some people who are recommending the transfer of the margin responsibility have precisely that in mind. They make no bones about it.

The Brady commission itself certainly makes no such arguments. In fact, it makes no attempt to relate its recommendations about margins in any way to the detailed analysis in its study. The Brady report simply refers, both directly and implicitly, to the famous Federal Reserve staff study of 1984 and calls for making margins consistent between markets.

We agree, but only to a point. Why not make margins consistent the easy way by taking the Federal Reserve out of the picture altogether? The New York Stock Exchange already controls everything about the margin process except the initial margins. Certainly the Federal Reserve does not believe that its control over the initial margins is a major weapon in the arsenal of monetary control. It set the initial margins on stock at 50 percent in 1974 and has kept them there for the past fifteen years.

Finally, there is the matter of circuit breakers. This is always an emotional issue, particularly with economists. By now, though, the discussion is virtually moot. Both the exchanges have implemented circuit breakers. The New York Stock Exchange has imposed a new rule that pulls the plug on the DOT computer system after a fifty-point move in the Dow. The Chicago Mercantile Exchange has imposed a limit of a fifteen-point move in its Standard and Poor's contract, a modified opening procedure, and some other minor adjustments that also qualify as circuit breakers.

I believe that the limits that have been imposed by both exchanges are much too narrow. But they will have performed a service if they succeed in forestalling efforts to "fill the regulatory void," as they so quaintly put it in Washington. We should proceed cautiously, since we are still paying the price of many ill-conceived regulatory void fillers devised in the 1930s and 1940s, such as the uptick rule and the insidious, though lesser-known, IRS short-short rule. The latter effectively keeps mutual funds from taking the other side of portfolio insurance futures trades.

It is important to keep in mind that we are no longer king of the hill in world capital markets. The foreign share of the financial services and futures industry has already grown substantially in recent years and will continue to grow. We cannot stop that, but we can certainly accelerate it with ill-conceived regulation.

Joseph Grundfest

Commissioner
Securities and Exchange Commission

Like the Brady report, the SEC staff study has been the subject of substantial criticism. The debate over the merits of each of the reports on the crash is, I believe, quite healthy. After all, the events of October 19, 1987, were unprecedented and complex, and in order to regulate the markets properly regulators must first understand the market.

The regulatory process, however, often operates on a schedule that is incompatible with careful analysis. More dangerous, perhaps, is the tendency for policy makers to fall prey to a peculiarly political form of cognitive dissonance. Indeed, in Washington, it sometimes seems that virtually any event can be cited as a reason for adopting almost any policy.

Consider, for example, the massive budget summitry that occurred in the wake of the market's October decline. The federal budget deficit, as dangerous as it may be from a macroeconomic perspective, was not the proximate cause of the market's fall. All rational evidence suggests that reducing the deficit would not help reduce the market's recent volatility. Nonetheless, political Washington rallied around the theory that the deficit caused the crash and that the budget gap had to be closed in order to restore calm and confidence to the nation's capital markets.

The reason for a quick consensus on such an obviously shaky proposition is clear. Many policy makers were unhappy with the formulaic budget cuts that would have been imposed under the Gramm-Rudman-Hollings bill. The market crash provided a convenient cause célèbre around which policy makers could rationalize efforts to renegotiate budget cuts without directly attacking the Gramm-Rudman mechanism. The theory that the budget deficit caused the market crash thus did not have to be correct in order to be widely accepted and immediately acted upon. Instead, the theory was accepted because it provided a convenient rationalization for actions policy makers wanted to take anyway. From that perspective, if the crash had not happened, some Washingtonians would have been hard pressed to invent its equivalent.

The lesson of the budget summitry experience is that the policy process, if not carefully monitored, can be manipulated to yield results that are inconsistent with any logical analysis but that serve some other politically valuable purpose. Thus, in the political arena, the most effective rallying cry may not be the most logical or analytically correct proposition; instead, it may be the theory that leads to the most politically sustainable conclusion, regardless of the evidence.

Despite the danger that logical analysis may have little sway over the final resolution of events, I remain an optimist that, at the margin, reason can help tilt the balance toward a more procompetitive resolution of the market's problems. In particular, I think it important that government recognize that two categories of events contributed to the decline on October 19. The first category encompasses events beyond the government's control. The government cannot effectively write or enforce rules that control investor psychology or dictate the way investors react to fundamental changes in the economic environment. Any such efforts are bound to be self-defeating and expensive.

Efforts to control trading strategies such as portfolio insurance fall into this category. Portfolio insurance is, in essence, little more than an elegant set of rules for stop-loss selling in a declining market. Stop-loss selling has been with us for decades, and there is nothing the government can do to prohibit investors from thinking about the market in a particular way. The government can, however, increase trading costs, and that can induce people to change their strategies, although it may not change the way they think about the market.

In all candor, some purchasers of portfolio insurance may not have correctly understood the limitations of that trading strategy. Evidence suggests that some institutional investors may have believed they could be heavily invested with little risk when the Dow stood at 2600 or 2700, even though they thought the market was overvalued, because they believed they could automatically get out before the market dropped too far. They apparently did not understand that a dynamic hedging strategy works well only in a smoothly declining market with sufficient liquidity. If too many traders try to implement the strategy at once, thereby overloading the liquidity in the market, or if the market gaps for any reason, portfolio insurance would not work as many expected. In effect, these investors acted as though they had purchased a synthetic put for which they had to pay no premium. Unfortunately, that is a bit like believing in the financial equivalent of a free lunch, and on October 19 the waiter showed up with the bill.

The second category encompasses events within the government's control and about which the government can do something. This category can be further subdivided into measures that can expand the market's capacity by increasing liquidity and improving information flows, and measures that slow the market down by throwing sand in the gears in any one of a number of ways. A great deal of effort has already been invested in devising more clever ways to shut the markets down when, for whatever reason, policy makers don't like the prices the markets are generating. Personally, I am more interested in focusing energy on efforts to improve market capacity, enhance liquidity, and generate better information because, in the long run, the effective survival of our domestic financial services industry depends on these measures much more than on any circuit-breaker mechanism, no matter how well designed.

The liquidity problems experienced during the week of October 19 were quite severe, and it is important to recognize that the roots of that problem stretch back at least two decades. In the late 1960s and early 1970s institutional investors began trading large blocks of individual companies' shares. The specialists simply did not have the ability to move 100,000 or 1,000,000 shares of a company's stock in a single block without seriously upsetting the market price. This problem was resolved through the evolution of block trading procedures that effectively created a joint venture between upstairs block traders at the large brokerage houses and the specialists on the floor of the New York Stock Exchange. In effect, upstairs traders shop large blocks by searching for other investors who are willing to take the opposite side of the transaction. This system is able to move larger blocks with a smaller price effect than would have been possible simply by walking up to a specialist and saying, "Guess what: here are a million shares to sell, have a nice day!" To move that million-share block the specialist would have to bang the daylights out of the stock's price by offering concessions that, as a practical matter, might not have to be made by the upstairs traders who can shop the block more effectively.

Today, however, a block is not composed of a million shares of a single company's stock. Today's million-share block is composed of a portfolio of 2,000 shares of 500 different companies. The New York Stock Exchange did not develop a marketing system that allows institutional investors to move these portfolio blocks at relatively low transactions cost. The failure of the NYSE to respond directly and effectively to this change in the demand for trading services created a tremendous opportunity for the Chicago markets. Chicago innovated when New York did not. It developed a cheaper and better market for the trading of portfolio block positions.

Interestingly, after extensive conversations with market participants, I think it accurate that many of the largest institutional users of the futures markets really do not care that they are transacting in futures. They would be just as happy to trade in the underlying equities if transactions costs in the equities market were as low. In other words, it is not the "futurity" of the futures market that attracts institutional interest; instead, it is the fact that futures markets provide the most effective and cheapest means of reallocating equity market risk. Until the equity markets address this problem head-on by creating an effective and low-cost means of trading blocks that are composed of diversified portfolios, the equity markets will be at a distinct disadvantage in providing liquidity to the portfolio trader.

Progress can also be made on the clearance and settlement side of the market by improving information flows among market participants. On October 20 in particular, because of delays and breakdowns in the settlement and clearance mechanism, there were occasions when the market did not have accurate information about the creditworthiness of some key market participants. This information failure caused some traders to refuse to do business with firms that were, in fact, quite solvent. This, in turn, removed liquidity from the markets at a time when the markets were desperate for all the liquidity they could find.

Information problems also severely hindered traders' ability to participate in the markets. At times, traders had difficulty estimating the prices that were actually available in the markets. They also had serious difficulties obtaining accurate information about the execution of orders that had already been entered. Trading is a risky business in that kind of an environment. Rather than deal with that degree of uncertainty, some traders just withdrew from the market, again removing much-needed liquidity. Others brave enough to trade demanded price concessions to compensate them for the information risks they were assuming, and on the 19th that generally meant making transactions at ever-declining prices.

As for the jurisdictional disputes currently embroiling the markets and regulators alike, I think there are far better uses of everyone's energies. Throughout the policy debate, New York has been busy pointing its finger at Chicago, and Chicago has been busily pointing its finger back at New York. Realistically, none of our markets covered themselves with glory on October 19. It behooves each marketplace to begin its analysis not with a criticism of its competitors' flaws—regardless of how reasonable such criticisms may be—but with some self-criticism aimed at addressing the fundamental problems revealed in their own back yards as a result of the extraordinary volume and volatility experienced during the week of October 19. I have already suggested that the stock exchanges can profitably consider new methods of transacting block trades that are composed of portfolio positions. The futures markets might also want to consider changes in their rules that limit the extent to which upstairs traders can prearrange trades. These restrictions may have adverse consequences on liquidity similar to those that result from the inability to trade equity portfolio blocks in the upstairs market.

As for jurisdictional disputes among the regulators, I would offer a couple of observations. Although some have suggested that the Federal Reserve be established as a super-regulator over the securities and commodities markets, the Fed apparently does not want the high honor, privilege, and responsibility of overseeing every financial market in America. As for the suggestions that the SEC take over responsibility for stock index futures from the CFTC, I think it important to recognize that any such shift would also entail a substantial reallocation of authority among powerful congressional committees. For the same reason that you would not want to fight a land war in Asia, I think you would not want to fight that jurisdictional battle on Capitol Hill. Although I understand—but do not necessarily agree with—the reasons many observers argue that jurisdiction over index products should be allocated to the SEC, we are not writing on a blank slate, and I do not believe any of those arguments are powerful enough to overcome the political realities of the matter. Since we are constrained as policy makers to deal only with realities, the proposal to reallocate jurisdiction strikes me as a nonstarter. Thus, rather than spend a lot of energy on a fruitless exercise, it makes far more sense to devote energy to good-faith attempts at interagency cooperation within existing jurisdictional constraints. That approach is, I think, the most responsible course of action open to regulators today.

Robert Davis

Commissioner
Commodities Futures Trading Commission

I certainly agree with Joe Grundfest that if you look at all the reports
you can find something in every report to agree with, and something
in every report to disagree with. You will also find a subset of recommendations common to all the reports. That should not be surprising.
These reports were prepared simultaneously, very quickly, and with
many of the same facts at hand. In those areas where all the reports
agree, a major mistake is much less likely to be made in a regulatory
policy recommendation. It is hard to imagine that all those reports
contain the same mistakes.

First, let me concentrate on some of those areas of agreement.
They primarily have to do with the ability of people in the system to
understand what is happening during major market events. Banks
must be able to understand the creditworthiness of people they have
to lend to. Banks have to be able to look into the system and have
information from clearinghouses or clearing members, so that they
are in a position to make proper credit judgments. It is not sufficient
during a crisis for the Federal Reserve simply to turn on the spigot.
The Fed does not tell banks to whom to lend. The banks still must
make credit decisions. During periods of illiquidity, if the banks do
not have the necessary information, or if there are uncertainties or
rumors about solvency, the system will not work very well. One of
the common points in all the reports is the need for more information
available in the system so that the proper decisions can be made.

Second, the reports have recommended that clearing systems
also need to be coordinated. One of the most interesting things about
October 19 and 20 was that huge intermarket transfers of funds
needed to take place. The unprecedented volume of transfer was the
sand in the mechanism. Nobody anticipated the amount of money
that had to flow from one place to another in the clearing mechanisms. There were informational failures and problems with the flow

of funds. All of the reports recognize these problems and look for ways to make the system stronger.

Let me quickly summarize a few observations that come directly from the analysis in the CFTC's report. First, there was no cascade on October 19. As it has been described in the press, the cascade theory implies an interaction between the stock market and the futures market so that both markets decline to some artificially low price. The price level that results is an aberration rather than a reflection of fundamental values. Our evidence suggests that there was not a cascade. For one thing the evidence is very convincing that the market decline was not a technical trading aberration. Had it been, the market would have returned to something close to its previous value, and it obviously has not. It seems, instead, to have settled into a new trading range of 1900 to 2000 on the Dow.

The market may have overshot on October 19 because of breakdowns in market-making mechanisms and liquidity problems. I do not discount some overshooting during the type of situation we experienced on that day, but the market seems to have adjusted to a new and much lower trading range.

Also in support of the argument that no cascade occurred is the fact that the futures index was reflecting the stock market after one adjusts the stock price data for the problem of nonsynchronous trading—the problem of stale data being reported in the Standard and Poor 500 series. There were no huge discounts in the futures market on the morning of October 19 that would have led to significant arbitrage selling on the stock market, selling that would have driven the stock market down and repeated the process over and over in a mechanical way. Instead, the futures market reflected about where the stock market was during that period, at least until index arbitrage broke down because of system failures and other types of institutional restraints. When these happened, of course, the cascade could not have occurred since it depends on arbitrage between the two markets.

An important point to remember, and this point was recognized in the SEC report, is that the futures market is a price discovery mechanism for equities. While that is not particularly surprising, certainly not to an academic, I view with alarm the problem that the SEC staff had with futures markets and equity index contracts being part of a price discovery mechanism. That is an appropriate function. In fact, it is one of the primary functions of futures markets.

If you cannot trade stocks and there is a price proxy that is designed to be a temporary substitute for baskets of stocks, then people who want to change equity positions will go to that market. If that market is available in a more or less continuous fashion, there is going to be price discovery in addition to what is happening at the New York Stock Exchange or at other exchanges.

We need a great deal of change in terms of market-making capacity. The most important problem is related to the liquidity available for selling baskets of stock. I am not referring to futures trading here; I am referring to trading baskets of stock. On October 19, roughly 40 percent of all basket trades involved futures-related strategies, whereas the other roughly 60 percent involved other types of basket trades.

There is an asymmetry with respect to the market-making mechanism available for baskets of stock and for individual stocks. If I want to trade a big block of IBM, there are several ways I can proceed. I can send it directly to the specialist post, or I can use the upstairs trading mechanism. This amalgam of the specialist and the upstairs trading may have come about in an ad hoc way, but it does bring a lot of liquidity to the market. You have the capital of the big trading houses available. Information about the block is simultaneously available, and the market can be made.

Basket trades, however, do not generally take place upstairs. If they go through the DOT system, as many do, they get divided into more digestible bites and loaded back-to-back so they essentially hit the specialist posts at the same time, where they hit only the liquidity available from the specialists.

The people at Salomon Brothers or Kidder or Morgan Stanley will tell you that they cannot respond fast enough to bring their liquidity to bear. Sometimes, in fact, they do not even know exactly what portion of trading is individual big blocks and what portion is program trading. For basket trades we are not even using all the liquidity that is available in the system now. It seems to me that is an important flaw. We need not only to make the cash market more liquid for basket trades, but also to improve the use of the liquidity currently available. This issue has not been addressed as completely as it should have been, although the New York Stock Exchange is exploring ways to facilitate the trade of baskets of stock.

From a policy perspective, one of the first things that occurs to me is that price change and, hence, volatility are obviously necessary to market processes. You cannot have market adjustment and you cannot have fundamental values reflected unless there is an ability to trade—unless prices change and there is some volatility.

What we want to do, if possible, is to identify different sources of volatility. In a sense, there can be "good" volatility and "bad" volatility. If the exchanges, the self-regulatory organizations, the trading institutions, and the regulators can identify structural situations that

29

lead to excessive volatility, then it would be appropriate to make changes designed to reduce that volatility.

It is also true that it is difficult to distinguish between volatility that is good and volatility that is excessive. For that reason, I have to come to the conclusion that if we cannot readily distinguish good from bad volatility, then it may be appropriate to establish some type of predictable mechanism that might come into play when the market moves to extremes. That is one thing price limits do. Other market mechanisms might do the same thing. But if you put a price limit in effect, when you run up against that constraint, you have essentially said that you do not know whether this is an equilibrium price movement or not, but the system cannot cope with any larger movement in this period.

Even if we are moving toward an equilibrium, it might make sense, in certain circumstances, to slow that process down. Economists have a hard time with that proposition. But we have seen the people that run futures exchanges rely on certain types of price limits for virtually the entire history of futures exchanges. This has not been imposed by regulators in Washington. Instead, this has been imposed by the people who run the markets in their own self-interest. So I have to conclude that there is some rationality to that decision.

I cannot dismiss out of hand what the Brady commission referred to as circuit breakers. I can only say that as a regulator in Washington, I do not have a clue what the appropriate market level is. When is a market move so extreme that it is disruptive to market behavior? When is a market move just something that worries everyone but ought to be allowed to continue? These questions are not ones that regulators in Washington really have very much insight into.

This brings me to my final observation with respect to these particular policy concerns. We are talking about restraints that we collectively want placed on us at certain times. These constraints should be constructed in a way that they are not damaging to the marketplace, so that they come into play rarely and in a predictable fashion. To the extent that regulatory changes are imposed on the marketplace, those are the characteristics we ought to be looking for.

Yet I see many proposals that seem to be designed to limit the market at all times. The suggestions about margin regulation fall into that category. What these proposals in fact do is to impose a dead-weight loss on market activity at all times, and the positive impact they might have during periods of crisis is minimal. During a crisis, when people are scrambling for the exits, it does not make much difference whether margins happen to be 15 percent or 20 percent or 50 percent. Investors are heading out the door. Those constraints do not have much impact during periods of crisis. But during normal times—99.9 percent of the time—excessive margins impose a dead-weight loss on the market. There is a loss in terms of trading activity and a loss in liquidity to market. It is a loss to every institutional investor, every participant in a mutual fund, and every person vested in a pension plan in the United States.

A report in the *Wall Street Journal* suggested that there may be a major impetus in Congress to impose the type of dead-weight-loss solution I have just mentioned. When I read that report I wondered what it would be like to raise my small children overseas. If we develop a regulatory response that restricts economic freedom in the United States and the opportunities exist elsewhere, that is where the markets are going to end up and most likely where I will end up also. So from the standpoint of my own family, I hope we avoid the extreme regulatory responses to economic events that we got in the 1930s.

Franklin Edwards

Columbia University

I want to step back a bit and try to put the various studies in perspective. Each was originally commissioned to determine what caused the crash. After some 2,000 or 3,000 pages the answer is, we still do not know what caused the crash. Much has been said about speculative euphoria, excessive price-earnings ratios, and the like. But the bottom line is that no one knows. Federal Reserve Chairman Alan Greenspan put it well when he said it was an accident waiting to happen. If it had not happened now, it would have happened later.

Did futures cause the crash? All the studies basically agree that the answer is no. The possible exception is the SEC staff study, which says that although futures did not cause the crash, it may have been sharper and gone further than it would have without futures markets. No evidence is presented on this point, but the suggestion is there that the futures markets played a role. But even the SEC study begins by noting that it does not address the question of what caused the crash.

Are futures markets valuable? All the studies say yes. I do not think that there is any quarrel about that. These markets provide valuable financial services—hedging and price discovery.

Given those conclusions, how do we make any sense of the fact that the studies go on for pages and pages and make recommendation after recommendation to change things? The explanation might be that it takes a brave commission to study a subject for two or three months and say, we do not have any recommendations.

What do they do? They focus on two problems illuminated by the crash: one, the disorderly conditions that existed in the markets and two, something that did not happen but could have happened—a 1930s kind of collapse.

By disorderly markets, I mean conditions under which orders were submitted but not executed and were sometimes returned for no reason at all; prices that were fictitious or wildly out of line; and opening prices on the New York Stock Exchange that had no relation to reality. No one likes to see disorderly conditions. What followed, therefore, were in-depth studies of what caused them.

The second issue was the potential for financial collapse—the fear that clearing associations might have collapsed and that we might have had an economic catastrophe. This is the basis for the recommendations to unify or coordinate clearing mechanisms.

My reaction to these studies is a little bit like being transported back in time. Suppose it is 1910 and the modern automobile drops out of the sky, landing right in front of us. Just to be on the safe side, let us suppose it is a Mercedes. It does everything well. It is fast and very safe; it has a powerful engine and good brakes. But of course in 1910 we do not have the roads to handle that kind of automobile.

We have a dilemma. The Mercedes is much better than the Model T, but what are we going to do about it? One thing we could do is to ban all modern automobiles. Fortunately, none of the studies went so far as to suggest banning futures markets.

The other thing we could do is to restrict the use of the modern automobile, on the grounds that it is dangerous. If we did not have adequate roads, all those modern automobiles might crash into one another. We could say, for example, that only certain people can use the modern automobile. By analogy, we could restrict the use of futures markets by imposing high margins or possibly even requiring physical delivery. In other words, we could find ways to make the costs of using this product so high that it would only be available to a few people.

Another way to limit the use of the modern automobile is to restrict speed. For futures markets we could say, by analogy, that you cannot use the DOT system to trade baskets of stocks; it is too fast. Or we could impose the uptick rule on futures, so that when prices are declining, futures cannot be sold. In other words, slow it down—impose a speed limit. Or we could say that every hour on the hour, cars have to stop moving for fifteen minutes. Similarly, we could impose circuit breakers on markets.

The other thing we could do, of course, is to build better roads (or market-making systems) to take full advantage of the capabilities of the modern automobile (and of futures markets and other derivative markets). What surprises me about many of these studies is that this is the one option that they do not explore.

The emphasis of these studies is on how to curb this new invention "futures," which we all agree is good but which cannot be handled with our present road system. We should not be thinking that way. We should be thinking about improving the roads so that we can use the modern automobile to its fullest capacity.

We need better market-making systems. The time has come to say that quite possibly the specialist system is out of date and not capable of handling portfolio trades.

I do not mean to restrict this criticism to the specialist systems. All our market-making systems should be carefully examined to see whether they are capable of handling the kind of modern trading we have. If they are not, how can they be changed? How can we have better information about the potential buy-and-sell orders and the limit orders on the books so that new buyers and sellers can come into the market as they are needed?

Much of the disorder on October 19 and 20 was in SEC-regulated markets—the New York Stock Exchange and the options exchanges. This suggests that there may be something in the SEC rules or in the market-making systems being used by these exchanges that can be improved.

In the rush to make recommendations, each of the studies fails to distinguish clearly between self-correcting problems and problems that might not be self-correcting. If we are going to impose new government regulations, they should be limited to cases where the self-interests of private market participants are not correctly aligned with the social interests—in other words, where there are externalities of some kind. The studies do not distinguish between recommendations to institute physical delivery instead of cash delivery, raising margins, tampering with the clearing associations, and curbing portfolio insurance.

But many of the problems revealed during the crash are quite clearly self-correcting. Mistakes were made. Sometimes you need a crash to illuminate weaknesses. The first ones who ought to know about the weaknesses and who have a stake in fixing them are those who have something to lose by their continued existence. Many of the problems identified will be automatically corrected.

There are also problems that may not be self-correcting, such as the market-making system. It seems to me that strong interests are involved in preserving the specialist system and resisting changes in the market-making systems in general. If there is an area of potential public policy interest, it may be in prodding exchanges to take a close look at their market-making systems to determine whether they are capable of handling the trading we have today.

PART TWO

Regulatory Issues

Thomas Coleman

Vice President and Director of Economic Analysis and Planning
Chicago Board of Trade

I am going to discuss margins primarily, and leave to others the discussion of limits and circuit breakers.

If one were to set up an ideal margin system, there are at least four criteria that would be important in evaluating the adequacy of the system: (1) Does the margin system provide enough money relative to the function it serves? (2) Does the system properly time the collection of that money? (3) Are the proper mechanisms in place for enabling that money to be collected? (4) And does the margin system self-adjust to changes in the market? With these criteria in mind there are several points about the futures margin system that I would like to discuss.

First, it is vital to keep in mind the function of futures margins. They reflect a performance margin concept, not a credit margin concept. There is no credit extended, so the collection and flows of money do not lead to credit consequences; rather, they lead to flows of money to cover risk for one day. The margin system is built around the concept of one day's price risk in a futures position.

Second, with futures margins, money is paid in advance. An initial margin must be posted before a position is even taken, and clearance is the same day. This contrasts with the securities margin system, where money is not required until seven days after the trade is made, and clearing takes place five days after the trade is made.

Third, futures markets have a unique clearing system with financial guarantees and risk analysis. It is not just a customer that puts up money; there is also a clearing member backing every customer. That clearing member provides a financial guarantee that it will put up the money if it cannot be collected from the customer. In addition, a clearinghouse is organized to oversee funds collections and to analyze the risk in the system. It is a multilayered system with many built-in backups.

Fourth, there is daily settlement, a pay-as-you-go concept. At the clearinghouse level, this means payments are made the same day in cash. At the Chicago Board of Trade, variation margin—money collected based on the price change in the position from yesterday to today—is actually collected twice a day, once in the morning and once in the afternoon. All variation margin is paid at the clearinghouse level in cash. If there is any question about the risk involved, that cash collection can be made on as little as an hour's notice.

Fifth, there is a continuous review of the levels of margins in the futures system, and changes are routinely made. The margin system at the Board of Trade generated over 200 margin changes in 1987. Margin levels are fine tuned to balance the cost of tying up too much capital and the security of having risk adequately covered.

To illustrate how the system works, I cite an example based on the week of October 19, 1987, and a few surrounding days when the margin system was under the greatest stress. I will use a position in the major market index since that is the contract traded at the Board of Trade (see table 1).

Consider what the dollar movements and the margin activity would have been in a futures position held in the major market index against an equivalent purchase of a basket of the same stocks that are part of the major market index. If this futures position had been purchased on Wednesday, October 14, at a price of 494.50 points, or $123,625, an initial margin of $4,500 would have been paid to establish the position. By the end of the day, the loss would have been another $4,500. So a total of $9,000 would have to have been put on deposit by Thursday, the following day.

In contrast, on the securities side, there would be no requirement for money to be paid in. Clearing of that trade would wait for five days. Collections of money would not be required for seven days.

Further market drops on Thursday would have resulted in another loss of $2,350, and the accumulated margin payment by the opening of trading on Friday would have been $11,350.

On Friday, when the market went down severely, $5,525 would have been lost. The cumulative total paid on the futures position, due by the opening of trading on Monday, would have risen to $16,875. The securities side position would still have no money paid in; it would be several days away from clearing and several days away from receiving the money required.

By Monday, when the record drop of 508 points in the Dow occurred, the position would have changed in value by another $27,125. Thus by Tuesday morning, market losses over the previous four-day period, coupled with a margin increase implemented by the

TABLE 1: MARGIN COMPARISON: ONE FUTURES CONTRACT POSITION OF THE MAJOR MARKET INDEX (MMI) COMPARED WITH ONE STOCK PORTFOLIO POSITION OF MMI COMPONENT STOCKS

October 14–23, 1987	Closing Market Value of Position (dollars)	Daily Change in Value of Position (dollars)	Futures Margin Account			Stock Margin Account	
			Accumulated paid-in margin at opening of trading (dollars)	Accumulated paid-in margin as % of day's closing market value	Accumulated paid-in margin as % of original purchase value	Accumulated paid-in margin at opening of trading	Accumulated paid-in margin as % of day's closing market value
Wednesday	119,125	−4,500	4,500[a]	3.78	3.64	0	0
Thursday	116,775	−2,350	9,000[b,c]	7.71	7.28	0	0
Friday	111,250	−5,525	11,350	10.20	9.18	0	0
Monday	84,125	−27,125	16,875	20.06	13.65	0[d]	0
Tuesday	91,125	7,000	46,500[e]	51.03	37.61	0[f]	0[f]

NOTE: One MMI futures contract was purchased on October 14, 1987, at a price of 494.50 points, or $123,625. One portfolio of MMI component stocks equal in value to one MMI futures contract was purchased on October 14, 1987, at the same level, 494.50 points.

a. Initial margin deposit of $4,500.

b. $9,000 = $4,500 initial margin deposit + $4,500 loss in value.

c. Position cleared; same day as transaction in futures, five days after transaction (Wednesday) in stock market.

d. Cumulative market losses of $39,500 for four days exceed the value of an initial 25 percent margin ($30,906), not required to be paid for four more days: loss October 14, $4,500; loss October 15, $2,350; loss October 16, $5,525; loss October 19, $27,125; cumulative losses, four days, $39,500.

e. Margin requirements increase to $7,000 from $4,500.

f. On the securities side, clearing would take place on the fifth day (Wednesday), but collection of the initial margin payment would not be required until the seventh day (Friday).

39

exchange, resulted in an accumulated paid-in margin balance of $46,500. On the securities side, clearing would not yet have occurred and money would not yet have been collected.

From the point of view of a securities broker looking at his risk in the position, the cumulative market losses at that point would amount to $39,500, or approximately 32 percent of the value of the initial position. The amount of money lost, not yet due for three more days, would exceed the 20 to 25 percent margin level specified in the Brady report as the margin paid by professionals. The money coming in on the stock side therefore would not be sufficient to cover the losses already incurred. Of course, if gains were experienced in the next couple of days, the deficiency could be at least partially made up. On the securities side, therefore, there would be reason for considerable worry about whether enough money would be available to cover the losses.

On the futures side, by Tuesday, cumulative daily payments in cash would have amounted to 51 percent of the value of the position on that day, or over 37 percent of the original position. The cash would be in hand, and the clearinghouse would be both collecting money and paying money out. There would be liquidity in the system for anybody who needed funds on the other side of trades to meet obligations somewhere else in these linked markets.

This example illustrates several important points. (The precise percentages are not important; they would be different for different days.) In the most extreme examples of negative market moves, the futures margin system collects money quickly; it gets it in cash, and it pays that money back out on the other side. That kind of system meets the criteria I set out initially for satisfying the needs of the marketplace in managing risk.

The press has commented frequently about a 50 percent stock margin versus a 10 percent or smaller futures margin. Clearly this amounts to comparing apples and oranges. There are many different margin levels on the securities side, depending on capital considerations and positions in the marketplace. This is also true on the futures side; the effective levels vary depending on what the market moves have been on the futures position. The quoting of any single percentage margin level in either system grossly oversimplifies the subject and distorts a genuine understanding of how margins work.

Hans R. Stoll

Vanderbilt University

As I reflect on the events of October 19, I am struck by the fact that those major price changes have not changed my views about the kind of structural changes we need in the stock market. There were structural issues to be addressed before October 19, and they are still with us. Many of those issues are illustrated by the volatility—though far less volatility than seen in October—associated with expiration days.

I would like to direct my comments to the issue of market linkages and circuit breakers. First, let me discuss the concept of "one market," a point that the Brady commission appropriately emphasized.

We can think of the concept of one market in various ways. One is that we have a worldwide communications system. In one sense that just means that people talk to one another. But in a broader sense it means there are links between related financial instruments traded in different physical markets. It means, in effect, that many physically separate markets are connected by arbitrage.

Arbitrage is critical to maintaining effective links among those physically dispersed markets. It is the mechanism that connects index futures to the cash market, currency futures to currency, and wheat futures to the spot markets for wheat. It is an integral element of the marketplace. And the arbitrage that connects index futures to cash is no different from the other kinds of arbitrage that we see in every kind of market. I am continually amazed by the criticisms of program trading and especially by the restrictions on program trading that have been imposed by the New York Stock Exchange.

We need to facilitate and improve program trading and index arbitrage and to find new methods of handling basket trading. We need more computer trading, not less.

Robert Whaley of Duke University and I have investigated the tightness of the links between the futures markets and the cash markets. We have looked at the minute-by-minute relationship of the

41

index futures prices to the cash index and to individual stock prices. We find that the futures market leads the cash market by about twenty minutes on average. It is obviously a variable lead. A good part of that lead is fictitious, since it simply reflects the slowness with which the component stocks of the Standard and Poor 500 trade. The futures reflect where the stocks will be when they trade, but the individual stocks take some time to trade.

An interesting result of our analysis is that even after controlling for that serial dependence in the index, we still find some lead of futures over the cash markets. Futures, in other words, are a quick way to trade. Futures prices would move before the cash prices even if all the stocks on the index were to trade at every instance. We also find no overshooting of futures prices. That is, we find that futures prices do not overreact and then come back. It is important to note that the lead has declined over time; the markets have become more closely linked.

I am concerned that restrictions on program trading and index arbitrage will increase the gap between the markets. That would be undesirable from the perspective of economic policy. It would be unfortunate if we introduced regulatory changes that weakened the link.

As a related matter, markets are becoming increasingly simultaneous rather than sequential. Historically, trading stocks has been a sequential process: you observe the price, you place an order, your stock trades, another order comes in, and everything gets funneled through one location. New York Stock Exchange trading procedures, for example, have been primarily sequential. But actual trading has become increasingly simultaneous in the sense that many upstairs trading offices are connected through worldwide upstairs communications links. There are now many market centers. One can trade equity options, index futures, or equities in many different markets around the world.

When activity becomes great, as it did on October 19, the trades are directed through a narrow funnel, resulting in considerable trading price uncertainty. You might place an order when the market price is 50. Your confirmation might come back with a trade at 40. Many orders are hitting the market, each assuming something about the current market price, each participant surprised when the confirmation comes back perhaps an hour later and the transaction price turns out to be very different from the market price at the time the order was placed.

How do we solve that problem? In situations where markets are overwhelmed, trading halts are appropriate when the order imbalances are large. When markets are simultaneous and many orders are coming in, the market price may be uncertain because of the great volume of activity. In those situations we cannot expect market makers to handle the volume of orders in the usual sequential manner. Even if they could, we cannot expect them to provide the necessary liquidity to bring the markets down slowly.

On these issues some lessons can be learned from expiration days. We had a similar phenomenon on expiration days when there were large order imbalances at critical points. The solution reached there—moving expiration to the opening, where there is a natural trading halt before the price is determined—has been a reasonable one.

I want to distinguish trading halts from closing the market. A trading halt is not closing the market. The price discovery process continues. We need a procedure for discovering the new equilibrium price. A price must be found at which buyers and sellers will come in on the other side.

The essence of a trading halt is that the market remains open in the sense that the price discovery process continues. Indications of possible prices should go out while imbalances are "publicly reported." That way market participants can see what is going on and make informed decisions about what to do.

Should trading halts be coordinated across markets? Not necessarily. If there is a structural problem in one market that makes a trading halt appropriate, it does not necessarily follow that a trading halt should be imposed on all other markets. Certainly related markets may choose to close, but that should not be imposed on them.

Should trading halts be coordinated across stocks? Yes, if the order imbalances are in baskets. We ought to have a procedure to determine whether they are in baskets or in individual stocks. There are trading halts in individual stocks now. But it is hard to tell whether the problem is in an individual stock or a basket of stocks.

If we think trading halts are a good idea, how do we do it? I am not a big fan of price limits, which are one option. When we have daily limit moves in futures, the markets close. It is more than a trading halt when the market closes. Everything stops; people go home and wait until they can start trading again. The purpose of a trading halt should be to accomplish a price change, not vice versa.

The Brady report commented on the low volume that produced a 500-point drop in the Dow. In fact, the best way to accomplish a 500-point drop in the Dow is with nearly zero volume. We want the price change without all the accompanying scurrying around and pressure on the market mechanism. If everybody thinks the price

43

ought to change, we should figure out what the new price ought to be and then let it change.

The idea of using trading imbalances and pressures as a basis for trading halts is a more reasonable one. The New York Stock Exchange roughly follows that procedure, although the party at interest, the specialist, has great influence in deciding when a trading halt should occur. The procedure needs to be more open, as does the procedure for reopening a stock after a trading halt.

Trading halts are not easy to engineer. The reopening problem is difficult. Finding the new equilibrium price is difficult. It involves iterations, trial prices, and the posting of imbalances, to give the market a sense of where it is heading. It is not easy, particularly when markets are disrupted and many things are happening. But it is worth thinking about.

Aside from trading halts, we should have other measures to enhance liquidity. We need to broaden the sources of liquidity in markets and the participation in providing liquidity. This has been happening over the years. The institutionalization of the market has moved much trading from the floor of the exchanges to upstairs offices. The stock exchange specialist system is also changing. Upstairs brokers are buying out specialists. Eventually, I suspect, more than one firm will be making a market in any particular stock. That is a healthy development. It will broaden participation and bring the upstairs firms into market making, not only for blocks where it already exists but also for baskets of stocks where it needs to exist.

Paula Tosini

Director
Division of Economic Analysis
Commodity Futures Trading Commission

I will comment briefly on margins and circuit breakers and will use as my point of reference the Brady commission report. If I had to use one word to describe that report, it would be masterly. The report deals with major issues, while leaving considerable room for significant differences in interpretation. People with widely different policy goals are embracing this document and using it as the basis for their arguments. I think the reasons for this are the adjectives used in the document, adjectives such as "coordinated" circuit breakers, and "consistent" or "harmonized" margins.

At present we do not have coordinated circuit breakers, at least as I interpret the Brady commission's idea of circuit breakers. If we have an overload in one section of a linked market, then we had better coordinate what breaks the circuit in that market with the circuit breaker in the other market, or else we are going to have a transfer of pressure. The approaches of the two markets are evolving, but they are certainly not coordinated at this time.

Futures markets have turned to their traditional means of dealing with price uncertainty, which is price limits. I do not think anyone in the futures market would say that price limits are good, per se. Most have described them as the least of several evils. But price limits serve a very useful financial purpose in that they allow the clearinghouse time to collect money.

There seems to be some misunderstanding about how price limits work. The futures market does not close when a limit is reached. People who want to transact at the limit price can; they are just not transacting at a market clearing price. If during the day, the market clearing price is within the range of the limits, then trading is resumed.

Price limits can also be quite flexible. In the latest proposals from

45

the Chicago Mercantile Exchange there would be lower limits early in the trading day and higher limits later in the day. They also have developed variable limits that change or even expire after one, two, or three days. There would not be any price limits on expiration days. Evidently, there is a range of experimentation even with price limits.

Price limits are a tradition in the U.S. futures market, even if not in the U.S. stock market. Japan uses price limits in its stock market, although admittedly Japan has a very different stock market and form of regulation.

As for trading halts, it is not at all in the tradition of the New York Stock Exchange to halt trading across the board. The traditional approach is limited to individual stocks, as a means of announcing imbalances. At present, when there is an imbalance, a new price range is announced. It is the best estimate by a floor official, working with the specialist, of where that stock will trade, given their knowledge of the imbalances and the situation at that time. Normally that price range is put out over the wires for at least fifteen minutes to bring in the other side of the trade.

On expiration Fridays at 9 a.m., after a natural overnight trading halt, the order imbalances are announced—so much net to buy or sell of market orders. Rather than giving a price, which is someone's imputation of the clearing price, the announcement gives the imbalance. This is perhaps a better piece of information since someone looking to take the other side now knows the size of the excess demand or excess supply of market orders.

As for coordinating circuit breakers, this has yet to be done. I do believe, though, that there will be movement toward the exchanges working together. We are not there yet. The market break, though, has imposed a revolutionary situation on top of evolutionary change. Two very different institutional environments are being brought together, and the speed at which the adjustment must be made has been greatly increased.

I share the concern of others that all futures markets that are functioning correctly are intimately linked to the underlying market, and that inhibiting arbitrage is not generally a productive enterprise. The Brady report, in fact, found arbitrage to be a necessary mechanism, a necessary bridge between the futures market and the cash market. Their conclusion was that after the arbitrage mechanism had broken down on October 19, the decline on the stock exchange was greater.

I think the Brady commission has raised the level of the debate on margins to a much higher plane. The focus is no longer on the 50 percent public margins, but rather on the fact that the futures market is a professional market. According to the extensive data we have on the markets from our large-traders' reports we know that approximately 70 percent of the S&P 500 futures open interest on October 19 was related to commercials. These include institutions such as broker-dealers and pension funds. Five percent or less are large speculators. The 25 percent that generally do not report to us are primarily small professionals who trade between two markets, such as spreaders between stock index futures and the options market.

With a professional market, what would consistent margins be? First, they would not be the 50 percent public margins. A better comparison would be the exemptions from the Federal Reserve Board's margins for specialists and professional broker-dealers. As the Brady commission correctly recognized, these professionals pay margins in the range of 20 to 25 percent, although sometimes margins can be as low as 5 or 10 percent. Basically, they pay a good faith deposit to ensure that there will be money available to pay the claims if there are any losses. In fact, then, we are not dealing with an issue of significantly different leverage between the futures markets and the stock market. Of course, one might question why there is concern with leverage. But accepting that concern for the sake of argument, the difference is not great.

A final point is that firms often have a futures market position as a complement to a cash market position. They are long the cash and short the futures, thus holding countervailing positions. The Brady commission recognized, as did the CFTC, that we must net the positions to evaluate firms' risk exposure properly. What is the leverage in a hedged position—a short futures position on top of a long position? Part of the reason for greater coordination or even common clearing is that when we know who is long the cash and short the futures then we can set consistent margins by looking at the net position. As we saw in the events of October 19, the vast majority of the futures positions were two-sided positions of that nature— hedged positions, arbitraged positions, or spread positions.

Richard Zecher

Treasurer and Senior Vice President
Chase Manhattan Bank

I would like to preface my remarks with two brief historical comments. First, whatever caused the market drop on October 19—and I do not have the answer to that question—it is certainly true that the drop was much more likely to happen in 1987 than in 1967. Most of our markets, including the stock market, the bond market, foreign exchange markets, and commodity markets, are far more volatile than they were twenty years ago. The frequency and the amplitude of movement in prices in these markets are vastly different from what they were twenty years ago. Most of the blame for the increase in volatility lies with the breakdown of the discipline on monetary and fiscal policies. In thinking about the events of October and trying to understand where we are today, we ought to keep in mind that this increased volatility in prices is what has driven the development of the new products and markets.

Second, there were major policy mistakes made at the time these new instruments were developed. Ten years ago the regulators at the SEC and at the CFTC gave a tip of the hat to what economists were saying about derivative markets—that they were part of the same market as the underlying security; that they were, in an economic sense, priced from the same information; and that we therefore had to think of the underlying market and the derivative market as a single unified market. Although a tip of the hat went to that concept, the rules and regulatory structure that were set up were quite separate for the different derivative instruments.

The concept of physically separating the markets and making different rules and regulations for key matters such as clearing, margins, and the rules that govern the exchanges led to the problems that we remember from the late 1970s. Remember the problems with front running (trading options in front of block trades) and tape racing (trading options before they were printed on the tape). The physical separation of these markets does not have much economic relevance. But the different treatment—the rules they function under, their clearing systems, and their margin systems—has caused many of the problems that we have seen over the years and are talking about today.

I agree with much of what has been said; so I will try to summarize the issues on which I have a somewhat different view.

While we use the word "margin" in the cash market and in the futures and options markets, margins perform different functions in those markets. I view margins in the futures and options markets as a substitute for credit judgment. That is to say, there are two basic ways in our economy to guarantee the performance of a counterparty in a financial contract. One is to devote a lot of resources to studying the creditworthiness of the individual. Credit is extended to that individual when there is an essentially unsecured exposure. That is what banks used to do.

The alternative way is to demand cash on the barrelhead. That is essentially what margins do in the futures markets and, to a lesser extent, in the options market.

The nature of margins in the cash market is very different. Margins were never conceived as primarily or even substantively designed to guarantee counterparty performance. In the 1930s the argument for margins was developed in terms of macrocredit allocation and as a way of slowing speculation. It was as if margin requirements would preclude people from borrowing money to buy stock.

Obviously, margins in the two markets are very different concepts. Academics and government analysts could make a real contribution by differentiating between the various uses of margins over the years. My feeling is that an arbitrary increase of margins to levels unrelated to the actual risks being borne by the counterparties would be counterproductive and detrimental to those markets.

Some modifications in margins would be desirable, however. If I create an overall position involving positions in futures, options, and cash on a variety of different exchanges, my positions should be offset against one another. That is, what I actually have to put up as margins should reflect my true exposure. This should be true for professionals on the floor, for institutional professionals, and for individuals. The way margin is now collected, if I put these positions on three exchanges, I would have an open position on three exchanges and face three different margin calls. I would face three margin requirements that would not be offset in the way they would if these positions were consolidated through cross-margining. There should be cross-margining. There should be consistent treatment of margins for a given economic position, regardless of how it is created.

I would like to see the thrust of the discussion on margins and any rule changes go in that direction. Cross-margining would have helped a great deal on October 19 and 20.

As to circuit breakers, I distinguish between the two kinds: the price limit and the trading pause. The trading pause is a good solution that is worth pursuing. It is not as arbitrary as a price limit, and it does not stop the price search process, which is critically important. This will become increasingly important as we continue trading twenty-four hours a day around the world. In this context I do not know what it would mean to have a price limit in a time zone. I will be trading in a few hours in Japan, Hong Kong, and Singapore. Then I will be trading in London. A price limit imposed in the United States will have little effect on what actually goes on, except to move business overseas.

Another problem with price limits is that, in practice they would contribute to a delinking of the futures markets and the cash markets, particularly in volatile periods. I feel very confident, from the history that I outlined earlier, that price limits cannot and would not be adequately coordinated.

Price limits would clearly affect the strategies that traders and portfolio insurers would follow. What is a trader going to do when a price is falling rapidly and approaching one of these price limits? He is going to try to get his orders in before the limit is hit. This would actually contribute to volatility.

One problem that we ran into on October 19 and 20 was unique to the options markets. At the Chicago Board Options Exchange one of the great problems caused by the large movements in prices was that the exchange was required to open new series of option contracts at each 5-point or 2½-point movement. By the time the opening rotation came around again, instead of a dozen series there might be thirty or forty series. Under this procedure one had to call out each call option and each put option and have the market makers seek a price that would open it.

Recently, this procedure was changed. As you would expect, the exchange learned from this experience and modified its rules accordingly. It will now open a few series and then price the rest of the opens off those prices. Traders can then trade the price up and down from the open.

Finally, two kinds of comments are coming out of the six studies concerning the use of the DOT system by arbitrageurs. One set of comments is very positive and builds on the idea of expanding the DOT system. This idea is resisted on the floor of any exchange, because it would divert some of the order flow away from the people who are standing there.

The other positive comments go in the direction of creating a spot market in indexes. The index market is very unusual. Virtually every other market that I know of began with a spot market. Then a forward market developed, then a futures market, and finally an options market. At this point there is a mature market. The index market, of course, developed in the opposite direction. It does not have a spot market, only a futures and an options market. The idea is to create a spot market in the index, which is not an easy thing to do.

The DOT system is one way to simulate that spot market and not a bad way. There are other ways to do it. We could create a certificate of some kind that would reflect the underlying basket of stocks and then allow trading in the certificate.

These are very positive suggestions, and they should be encouraged. I do not know whether they will work, but they should be considered.

The other set of comments, which are basically negative, deal with closing the DOT system, so as to limit access in certain circumstances. This would be extremely unwise.

Before closing, I would like to comment on the charge that the portfolio insurance product is fundamentally flawed in conception, as some have suggested here. The suggestion seems to be that buyers did not recognize the risks and did not understand the limitations of portfolio insurance.

We offer a portfolio insurance product at Chase that received wide attention last year as a new product. Actually it is a combination of two old products that look new when they are put together—a bank deposit with an interest rate tied to the S&P 500. If the S&P 500 rises, the customer receives more interest. If it falls, the customer receives his principal back. We use a combination of futures and options to hedge this product, but the hedge is not perfect.

We were skittish about introducing this product because we understand the risks. We felt that an event like the market break on October 19 could occur, was very unlikely, could lead to the cessation of trading totally, or could lead to a badly mispriced options market, so that the hedging instrument was mispriced relative to the position being hedged. As those events did occur, we were unable to effect the full hedge. We lost money. But the risks of portfolio insurance products were well understood, both by the people buying the product and by the suppliers such as Chase.

Keep in mind that portfolio insurance is generally sold to very

51

sophisticated investors, such as pension fund managers. They understand that markets can close. We are not confronted with lawsuits from our many customers—pension funds, primarily—even though the protection they received was less than they had hoped for. Chase has continued with the product, and we believe it is a good one. It has received good market acceptance. It remains a very safe way to invest.

PART THREE

A Futures Perspective

William J. Brodsky

President and Chief Executive Officer
Chicago Mercantile Exchange

Although everyone is reading the studies and their recommendations, I want to quote from the introduction to a study not many have read. It begins,

> We emphasize that although many specific recommendations for improvements in rules and practices are made in the report, the report demonstrates that neither the fundamental structure of the securities markets nor the regulatory patterns of the Securities Acts requires dramatic reconstruction. At the same time, the report makes very clear that important problems do exist, and additional controls and improvements are much needed. The tremendous growth in the securities markets over the last twenty-five years imposed strains on the regulatory system and revealed structural weaknesses.

That is from the special study of the securities markets in the American and New York Stock Exchanges in 1963. What does it say? As much as things change, they remain the same. And the term "block trading" had not yet been coined in the early 1960s.

Technology—whether in a Mercedes Benz or anything else—often runs ahead of the systems surrounding it and ahead of regulators and other governmental officials, whose understanding of what is happening in the markets may also lag. It is the job of all of us to make sure that something fundamental to the well-being of this country is not harmed.

I would like to discuss four areas addressed by the Brady commission and how the Chicago Mercantile Exchange is responding to the recommendations. The four areas are: clearing and settlement procedures, information flows, margin requirements and financial safeguards, and circuit breakers.

We believe that the Brady report was a very fair document.

Although we do not agree with every point, we think it was a professional job and, given the time constraints, a job well done. We have given it a lot of thought; we have taken some steps already; and, of course, we will take many more later.

Clearing and Settlement Procedures

We believe that there should be a coordinating group to work on the markets generally. Instead of a super regulator, as the study recommends, we prefer an intermarket coordination committee, which would be involved in clearing and settlement and financial integrity issues, as well as other aspects of market coordination.

This committee could be fashioned after something that already exists in the securities world, the Intermarket Surveillance Group. It grew out of the special study of the options markets in the late 1970s. That study recognized that the securities exchanges—particularly the New York Stock Exchange and the option exchanges such as the AMEX and the Chicago Board Options Exchange—were not talking to each other, although they were one market. The ISG brought people from these institutions together with the Securities and Exchange Commission to coordinate surveillance, and it has worked well.

We propose that all the relevant exchanges, as well as the SEC, the Federal Reserve, and the Commodity Futures Trading Commission, participate together, identify the issues, and provide coordination. We do not think another level of government is necessary to do what the private sector can do itself, with government involvement.

On the clearing side, the group could coordinate the pay and collect data used in daily settlements. We do that now on the futures side but not on the securities side. In regard to clearing, firms often have positions in the securities markets, say in stock options, and in the futures market with offsetting valuations, but have no one place to look at all their positions. We would use a concept that already exists, the Designated Self-Regulatory Organization, to keep an eye on the firm it is responsible for.

In short, a lot can be done in market coordination beyond ideas like circuit breakers. If this committee is properly composed, it could be a vehicle for working out issues on a regular basis as well as in emergencies.

Information Flows

The sharing of data would have helped significantly in October. We were doing on an ad hoc basis what could be done routinely.

The role of the Fed is very important when it comes to issues relating to money flows. This is one of the greatest contributions of the Brady report. Before the Brady report, the futures industry did its thing, and the securities industry did its thing, and the banks tied it all together. The Brady report pointed out clearly that there is one market. Liquidity became a very important issue—not financial safety, but liquidity, the money flowing back and forth. With the involvement of the Fed, this kind of structure could allow a good dialogue, an exchange of information.

The flow of information includes the idea of cross-margining, and that is a complicated issue. In theory, it has a lot of appeal, but in practice it is hard to do for technical, political, and other reasons. Cross-margining has been brought up as a result of these studies and should be pursued. We are now investigating it, very carefully.

On our own, we are dealing with other issues in the clearing and settlement process that could fold into the joint efforts. One is in bank settlements. We encountered specific problems in obtaining fund transfers during the crash that related as much to operational problems as to anything else. One of these problems, documented in the Brady report, was that the Fedwire in Chicago went down for two hours on Tuesday—the worst possible day. It resulted in rumors that our clearinghouse was in trouble when we could not move the money.

We are pursuing several possible solutions. We are amending our agreements with our settlement banks to clarify their responsibilities. We are working with the Federal Reserve Board to eliminate the lag between a bank's commitment to an exchange and movement of the money on the Fedwire.

The Fed should be commended for keeping the wire open longer than normal during that period because of the tremendous traffic. That shows why the Fed must be included in this process.

Margin Requirements and Financial Safeguards

On October 19, we had three interday margin calls requiring funds within one hour, which we do when markets make big moves. These calls and mark-to-market at day's end brought the amount of money we had on account to upwards of 40 percent of the value of the S&P contract. We learned, however, that we were asking for money from people who owed us money, but we were not giving any money until the next day to those we owed. We were therefore getting in more money than we needed, because that is the way the clearinghouses have worked.

57

We understand these issues better than we did before. We recognize that we can create a liquidity crunch in our zeal to do a good job for our financial integrity. If there is one market, then there has to be some symmetry to the cash flows.

Our proposal is to have interday margin calls on a much more regular basis. People will expect them in little more than minor moves, rather than only in major moves.

But we will not only take in money, but pay money out to those who have positions moving in our favor. That will reduce the liquidity crunch on the contra side. We are encouraging other clearinghouses and agencies to do the same.

We have increased our speculative margins to 15 percent, as an indication of the benefit of the concept of harmonization in the Brady report. But we are vehemently against the idea that the margins should be the same just for the sake of being the same. Different margins reflect different concepts that work differently. The amount of risk in the system on a five-day settlement cycle on securities is far greater than any in the futures market. It involves an enormous liability, with no money coming in for five days. On the security side, there isn't even a structure to ask for the money in most cases.

We recognize that margin is an important issue, but we also believe that our track record has been superb. To make margins the same, at some arbitrary number that is not required, even under Reg T, makes no sense. Our margins, while at 15 percent numerically appearing less than securities, are in fact quite high, but we will keep them there for the foreseeable future.

We are making changes, however, in other areas of risk. One is on option margins. Previously we figured option margins on a delta-based system, a system that had been used for many years in the options and futures business. But we are developing a system we call dollars at risk, a much more sophisticated computer-based system for measuring risks and getting the money in.

We have a net capital rule in the futures business that we think should be changed. We have worked with the other exchanges, as well as with the CFTC, and made a filing to base the capital rule on the risk of the positions. The traditional method is based on the amount of customer money on deposit.

Although we believe that our margins have been more than adequate, and our record has shown that, we are increasing the amount of money that has to be in a security deposit fund at our clearinghouse. That gives us liquidity.

We did not have a failure of a futures firm in October. In light of the liquidity issues that we learned about, however, we decided to increase the amount of security deposits that we will hold. We will have upwards of $50 million in our security deposit fund.

Circuit Breakers

On the issue of circuit breakers, on October 22 we imposed a price limit in our futures contracts, which at the time was the equivalent of about 250 Dow points. It was 30 S&P points. At that time, of course, the market was very volatile, but now, stepping back from it, we felt that was rather high.

For many reasons, price limits are undesirable. Institutions that are in the market and want protection need it most when we are turning it off, particularly when there is no corresponding circuit breaker on the security side. But, in his testimony before the Senate Banking Committee on the Brady task force recommendations, Alan Greenspan said: "Price limits and other circuit breakers must be viewed as inherently destabilizing, but they may be the least bad of all the solutions."

We are not happy with the idea of price limits, so we continue to grapple with this issue. If we come up with a coordinated concept that will perform similar functions, then of course we can review it.

We have what we think is an innovative approach. We have price limits in two aspects. First, we have a price limit based on the value of the contract, which would apply at all times. That would be equivalent to approximately 120 Dow points at the current levels, which is 15 S&P points. That would be the outer range of where this circuit breaker would cut in. Second, if there is a big move in the market in the first ten minutes of trading, we will have a much more narrow price limit—5 S&P points, which equates to about 40 Dow points.

We have done that because of our experience in October. There was no question that day in October that the equity markets were going to be down severely.

Futures provide a price discovery mechanism. In one transaction, our market is open. The stock exchange could take 1,500 separate openings before anyone really knows what the stock market is doing. Therefore we should narrow the band—because of what happened, and not because futures are not an effective price setting mechanism. People have told me that when our market opened that day, it was down the equivalent of 200 Dow points. In London, stock prices were down about 200 points. If we could take the prices of the stocks in the S&P index as they opened on the New York Stock Exchange—and it took hours for some of them to open—and if we could put together an opening price, it probably was down 200 points.

Ironically, our system worked very well. But, as the Brady commission said, it has a billboard effect. Since our market opens first, the world knows that the market is going to be down—in this example, 200 points. In the view of some, that creates the impression that the futures market is dragging the stock market down. I don't think that is the case. The analyses of expert economists confirmed that the futures market did not bring down the stock market. London and Tokyo showed that the stock market was going to be down.

We want a very narrow band, equivalent to 40 Dow points or 5 S&P points for the first ten minutes of trading. Since this is innovative, we will have to experiment with it. It is intended to limit the amount the market can move up or down when it opens, though we only seem to worry about the downside. After ten minutes, the New York Stock Exchange opening system normally gets into play.

We hope that this will give people an opportunity to assess the situation. People who had orders in the pit the night before may not be aware that the sentiment has changed and prices are dramatically down. If the market is in a "limit down situation," it gives brokers a chance to call their customers and ask whether they still want to buy.

We are also doing something in hedge exemptions. The bulk of our market from the public side is institutional. We allow pension funds, for example, and insurance companies and college endowments to have a position in our market that exceeds our speculative limit if it is a hedge. If it is a hedge, it is not a speculative position, so we allow those users a position speculators cannot have.

Before the crash in October, if an institution had a hedge exemption and needed to go beyond it, we would allow it to do so if it reported to us that day.

We have now decided not to allow that, in the new world we are living in. The hedge exemption is now a firm exemption in specific contracts. If the institution needs more, it must apply in advance. As the Brady report suggested, there is one market, so we should allow access to each component by institutions and users of other components.

There are artificial restraints on institutions using our markets. Since I ran options at the American Stock Exchange, I have campaigned to allow institutional access to derivative markets, and I think more can be done. The Investment Company Act, for example, prohibits mutual funds from placing futures margins with futures commission merchants, and state insurance laws prohibit institutions from using futures markets in certain respects.

On this point, the *Wall Street Journal* quoted James Martin, the executive vice president of the College Retirement Equity Fund

(CREF)—which probably has the biggest fund of equity capital in the United States. He said that if he could do index arbitrage, he would. "I think it's a perfectly honorable profession," he said. "If more of us did it, the opportunities would get smaller because more firms would be competing to close the same spreads. The product is a legitimate hedging product and a legitimate way to add liquidity to the market." This is not speculation; this is hedging in its purest sense. Yet, because CREF is considered an insurance company under New York law, they cannot do it. I think it is important to allow institutions equal access to all the markets.

There have been meetings in Washington of late between the CFTC and the SEC. I participated in one with the chairmen of both those agencies and the chairman of the New York Stock Exchange. There have also been recommendations, some of which we embrace, some of which others embrace, and, of course, some of which we all reject. But we all agree that we need more coordination and cooperation, and that we have one market.

One of the best examples of our spirit of cooperation relates to the problem of triple witching, which was a big issue in 1986. We met with the New York Stock Exchange because we recognized that Friday afternoon is a poor time for them to have 60 million shares dropped on the specialist books. The exchange would prefer to have the settlement of our contract at the opening of the market rather than at the close of the market. When some of our people asked what we were getting in return, we said that the institution that has to be part of the settlement believes it will do a better job. Now that we have gone through several of those settlements, we see clearly that we did the right thing. The SEC and CFTC did not have to prod us.

We believe that the private sector can work out many of the issues brought up in the Brady report and in others. The government can supervise if necessary, but the technicians in the marketplaces should work out the details.

International Competition

The CFTC and the SEC have worked for a good flow of information between our country and other countries, in particular between our authorities and authorities in the United Kingdom, in futures as well as securities. This is a step in the right direction. A similar move is afoot on the Japanese side. Although real uniformity of regulation may never occur, I think there is a desire to recognize not only that there is one market in the United States in stocks, stock options, and stock index futures, but that it is clearly a global market.

The governments in England and Japan work with industry in lock step, though not in disregard of the public interest. They view their role as to support the effort of business to compete with other countries. Our regulators and legislators must understand that this is the competition we face.

While we will see a certain level of communication, we must remember that we are competing in a global market. The major users of our market are also major users in Japan and in England. If the market is good, they will go after it. National boundaries will not matter.

The Tokyo stock exchange is already in the financial futures business. Two years ago, the Japanese started trading bonds on their long-term government debt. We call them yen bonds, the equivalent of our T-bonds. Just as the Board of Trade's Treasury bond contracts are the most actively traded futures contracts in the United States, the Japanese started a yen bonds futures contract. That contract trades as much in value as the Board of Trade bond contract, or more, and it is only two years old.

The Japanese financial community has an amazing capability to do things. A year ago, when we were in Japan to open the first office of any U.S. exchange in Japan, the Japanese government for the first time allowed their institutions to use our futures markets. That was a big plus for our community. At the same time they are moving to authorize the Japanese exchanges to have a cash-settled stock-index futures contract in Japan.

The biggest banks in the world are in Japan. The biggest brokerage firms in the world are in Japan. The biggest insurance companies in the world are in Japan. They want to get into the financial futures business. If we tie ourselves up in knots on issues of regulation or jurisdiction, we are going to see the markets that we invented and nurtured suffer under tremendous competitive threats. While we fight internally, the real competition will lie without.

While I support many of the recommendations and believe we are right to pursue them, I want to make sure we don't lose sight of the ball. There is a ball out there, called international competition, and if we do lose sight of it, we could be in real trouble.

PART FOUR

Trading Systems

John C. Coffee, Jr.

Columbia University

A common denominator in all the recent studies is the internal order of their argument. Each begins by discussing the new phenomena of stock-index arbitrage and portfolio insurance and then proceeds to explain the degree to which they did or did not cause or contribute to the market break in October. This line of argument ignores the possibility of other, larger factors that are more deeply rooted, more institutional.

Consider the following excerpt from the introduction to the SEC study, in a paragraph addressing negative market psychology:

> The knowledge, by market participants, of the existence of an active portfolio insurance strategy created, in our view, a market overhang effect in both the futures and stock markets. This resulted in the maintenance of futures discounts that discouraged institutional traders from participating in the stock market on the buy side, but discouraged specialists from committing capital to maintain fair and orderly markets, and to discourage block positioners from maintaining normal levels of activity.

In other words, the report asserts that these new trading strategies cause discounts in the futures markets, which have a variety of adverse consequences. My problem here is not with the possible existence of a negative market psychology or an overhang; it is with the presumed causality. It seems to me that the report has confused cause and effect. The truth may not be that stock-index arbitrage causes discounts in the futures market but that discounts in the futures market cause stock-index arbitrage.

While that seems to be true almost by definition, it leads to a bigger question: What are the more basic causes of the problem of discounts in the futures market? I note here, parenthetically, that the term "discount" is almost pejorative. Everyone seems to focus on discounts in the futures market, which they believe destabilize the other market. It might be better to talk about one market leading the other.

How can we explain the persistence of discounts in the futures market ahead of the securities market? In my view some obvious institutional factors have greater explanatory power than the popular "cascade scenario" or the "meltdown" rhetoric that has captivated the press.

First, there are much lower margin requirements and lower transaction costs in the futures market than in the securities market. Second, short selling is essentially unregulated in the futures market. This contrasts with the securities market, where the SEC has imposed the uptick rule, Rule 10a-1, which restricts short selling in a down market.

Third, the futures market has no specialist system, or, indeed, any substitute mechanism that seeks to cushion or break price fluctuations. Each of these factors tends to contribute to an environment in the futures market in which higher price volatility seems to be predictable.

Since the other panelists have already said a great deal about the first of these factors, margins, I will not cover that ground again. I would note, however, that the SEC report has a theory of margins— that lower margins lead to highly leveraged markets. Highly leveraged markets are susceptible to more rapid price declines because, when there is a margin call, larger positions must be liquidated and that leads to more selling pressure.

There are alternative theories. For example, the market psychology in the futures market may be very different from that in the securities markets. The futures market may be populated by risk preferrers. This is only a hypothesis, which I will not pursue.

I would like to focus on the second point, which has to do with the regulation of short selling in a down market. Under SEC rules in effect since 1938, short sales of securities can only be made when the last transaction at a different price was on an uptick. In other words, you cannot sell short if the market is declining or if there are level ticks between you and the last tick, which was also a downtick.

In contrast, selling a futures contract is similar to selling short a basket of securities. This form of short selling is not regulated. Moreover, the use of cash settlements simplifies the process of selling short by selling a future since one need not worry about borrowing stock to cover the short sell. One can settle in cash.

The futures market also lacks the specialist. However skeptical one may be about the performance of specialists, it is clear that they have an effect, at the margin, in retarding price movements. Hans

Stoll mentioned that the futures market leads the securities markets because of the longer period required to make the covering transactions in the 500 Standard and Poor stocks. Although it is true that it takes longer to execute these multiple trades, there is also a specialist sitting there who must try, even in a panic-stricken moment, to retard any price fluctuation. Hence, even without program trading, stock-index arbitrage, and the like, prices should move downward more slowly on the securities market than on the futures market.

To put it bluntly, the contrast here is between a "fair and orderly market"—to use statutory terms—in New York and an efficient but volatile market in Chicago. That contrast becomes particularly important when we turn to the issue of volatility. That is, the greater volatility on the futures market flows to the securities market through the mechanism of stock-index arbitrage. This flow-through is imperfect today largely because of the the barrier provided by the rules against short selling.

Consider, for example, the effect of the short-selling rule when the futures market is at a discount to the securities market, perhaps as a result of program trading. The appropriate arbitrage strategy would be to buy the cheaper futures and sell stock. Today, however, most traders cannot engage in this strategy because they have no assurance that the stocks will sell on an uptick. If the stocks turn down, which is exactly what we would expect if the futures market is leading the stock market, the typical trader would be caught in midstream, knowing that he cannot sell stocks short in New York without getting caught in an exposed, risky position.

Thus, to the extent that stock-index arbitrage works, at least in this setting where we are going to be short in stocks in New York and long in futures in Chicago, it works because we have some traders, typically index funds, who are already long in stocks. They have large inventories of stock that can be liquidated for a quick, almost riskless profit. The extent of such stock-index arbitrage is considerable and has raised the ire of other investors who believe that it is destabilizing the market.

My contention, though, is the reverse. There may be insufficient stock-index arbitrage, because it clearly has not fully eroded the futures discount. That is, the persistence of a futures discount suggests that the arbitrage mechanism is not working fully. One reason is that it works only through the mechanism of those, such as index funds and other institutional investors, who are long in stocks at the moment that the disparity between the futures and the stock market arises.

Some have argued that the huge discounts that persisted on

October 19 would not have done so if the short-selling restrictions had not been there to limit the ability of intermarket arbitrage to equalize the two markets. This point has been debated by others who point to technology and trading halts as also having played an important role, and I do not doubt that they did. But the possibly adverse effect of the restriction on arbitrage frames the policy issue that I want to focus on.

If we see the futures market discount as destabilizing, as suggested by the SEC report, one way to deal with it is to promote greater intermarket arbitrage by permitting pure short selling between markets where it is part of an arbitrage program. I am not referring to pure short selling. Nor am I talking about the person who is already long in stock, such as the institutional investor, but rather about the trader who wants to sell stock in New York and buy futures in Chicago in purely offsetting transactions so that, in our one-market concept, he is perfectly hedged. Under Rule 10a-1 there are certain small exemptions to the restriction on selling short in a down market, but they do not generally exempt arbitrage between the stock and futures markets.

As we move to the notion of one market, it will be important to recognize that a trader is not short, for purposes of the securities laws, if his integrated futures and securities holdings are perfectly hedged. This approach would open up room for a great number of traders not holding large stock positions to move quickly to equalize discounts between futures and stock markets.

Some may respond that equalizing the two markets in this fashion would trigger more program trading and bring down the stock market. The logic behind this assertion depends on the view that the futures market discount is harmful because it tends to inhibit the specialist and other traders from being active in the market and to create a potential for panic.

The policy choice is this: Do we want to eliminate the overhang effect of the futures market discount? Or do we want to maintain that discount and thereby prevent it from flowing through to the stock market and triggering more portfolio selling? What is the goal?

Those who oppose increasing the availability of intermarket arbitrage would hold the latter position. Build a dike, they argue, that prevents the overhang from flowing through by restricting any short selling even by a trader who is truly hedged in the total market.

In reply to that position I would say that we cannot have it both ways. Today we are at a halfway point that makes no sense. We have stock-index arbitrage as performed by index funds and other institutional investors, which can eliminate most of the futures discount. But this process is neither quick nor smooth. There is a huge population of other traders who could make the process quick and smooth if the law were different.

An intermediate position, which I am not necessarily advocating, deserves careful examination. If we are concerned about price volatility and short selling, perhaps we should think about the degree to which it might be appropriate to restrict the selling of futures on stock products when the person holding the futures position is not also long in stock. If you are really selling short when you sell a naked futures contract, are there any circumstances under which we should restrict this so-called short selling in the futures market? What I am referring to is applying the SEC's uptick rule to the futures market, coupled with an elimination of any restrictions on short selling as part of an arbitrage program. Such a rule would in no way restrict portfolio insurers because they are long in stock. It would, however, restrict volatility at its source, the futures market, which the SEC report describes as the price leader.

I am not suggesting that such a rule be adopted, but it needs to be on the list of options we look at to deal with price volatility. It is certainly preferable to building an artificial dike that keeps that discount in the futures market from adjusting the price in the stock market by restricting transactions between the two markets.

My own tentative conclusion is that there is not yet an adequate reason to restrict short selling in the stock market or selling of naked futures in stock index futures. The short-selling rules derive from our experience in the late 1920s and 1930s with bear raids. Bear raids are, by definition, firm-specific. A conspiracy forms to manipulate the price of a stock and sell it short, hoping to buy it later at a profit.

Although is possible to have bear raids in individual stocks—and if we had futures on individual securities, there might be a need for a similar uptick rule on the futures contract—it is very unlikely—indeed it stretches credibility to believe—that there can be a bear raid on the stock market as a whole. This is essentially what is required for there to be a bear raid on stock index futures that could justify the application of an uptick rule to them.

As to the specialist system, there is a curious circularity in the SEC report. It says repeatedly that nothing could have been done to stop the October market break but we must shore up the specialist so he can be unsuccessful again under similar circumstances.

What is the rationale for the specialist system? Are we trying to protect individual investors so as to keep them in the market? Individual investors may have already fled to mutual funds and other intermediary devices. Or are we protecting them by subsidizing an illusion, that is, that we can have a fair and orderly market? If so, we are making a mistake. If the SEC report is correct in its statement that the futures markets are the place where institutions now go to discover price, the securities market cannot be a fair and orderly market. If the futures market is the price leader, we cannot keep the securities market fair and orderly except by imposing arbitrary barriers between the two markets.

Let me apply this thought to a likely future development. There has been discussion of the New York Stock Exchange's opening its own post to trade some kind of stock-index product. Presumably such a post would have a specialist, who would trade the index product on the floor of the stock exchange.

If I am right, the specialist would have a hopeless task in the face of a futures market that moves faster and in large, discontinuous leaps.

Consider what would happen if we had a stock-index product in both Chicago and New York and prices fell. Assume that prices fell in Chicago first because of the differences in margins, in transactions costs, and in short-selling restrictions and the absence of a specialist. Arbitrageurs would buy in Chicago and sell in New York. Selling by arbitrageurs in New York would mean that the specialist would have to buy a tremendous amount of these indexed products. The amount of capital that could move in quickly to even out price disparities between wholly fungible products—two stock indexes, one in Chicago and one in New York—could drown any specialist. This is only a prediction, but it will be interesting to see what happens if the New York Stock Exchange does try to adopt a new index product and maintain the specialist system.

Let me close with two final comments about the specialist. One is sympathetic. I think we should recognize that, with the emergence of portfolio insurance, the specialist is subject to far more uncertainty than in the past. Portfolio insurance is in a sense an improved substitute for the old-fashioned stop-loss order. It is a strategy by which the holder of a portfolio can limit risk. In the past the stop-loss order was exposed to the specialist. He had the order before him, he knew the total structure of the market, and, he could act in light of it. Now he does not know how much selling pressure is coming and at what points. He knows the market is sticky and that there will be large amounts of securities coming in at various points. But he does not know where or when. No wonder the specialist does not like a market overhang. The remedy may be to give the specialist more information. Perhaps there should be some means by which the specialist is informed about the portfolio strategies that are in place and at what point institutions will begin selling indexed futures contracts to hedge their losses.

My other comment is that now that we have large investment banking firms acquiring the specialist position, we will face a new set of conflicts. One of the oldest rules in the securities law is Rule 10b-6, which says, in effect, that you cannot buy what you are selling in a distribution because it is inherently manipulative. There is a serious conflict of interest here. The stock exchange and the SEC have dealt with this problem by requiring a Chinese wall. I must say, not cynically but with some pessimism, that the past two years have not given many of us a great deal of confidence in the utility of Chinese walls.

Philip McBride Johnson

Partner,
Skadden, Arps, Slate, Meagher & Flom

The problem with commissioning studies of any major event is that they tend to imply that obvious answers should be discounted in favor of more exotic explanations. The studies of Black Monday—and I count no fewer than seven of them—have been especially faithful to that precept. The October 1987 stock market plunge has been attributed to at least a dozen causes and so-called exacerbating influences.

I am not sure I know what an exacerbating influence is. I suppose one could say that the survivors of the Titanic exacerbated the tragedy by not staying on board with their bailing buckets, but, oh, by the way, there was also an iceberg. When an elephant stands on my foot, it is not likely that I will attribute the pain to a vitamin deficiency or insufficient sleep or an anxiety attack. I will look down at my foot and draw the appropriate conclusion. My opinion, held with the conviction that only a person without economic or finance training could have, is that an elephant was present last October and remains in our midst today. More important, it is likely to hang around even if the markets are purged of program trading, portfolio insurance, specialists, stock indexes, unreliable computers, or any of the other targets of criticism.

On October 19 and 20, 1987, about 1.25 billion shares of stock changed hands on the New York Stock Exchange. I did not sell any shares on those days, and chances are neither did most people. Similarly, program trading and portfolio insurance were prevalent then. I do not know about others, but I have never engaged in either of those activities. But clearly someone did.

So allow me to introduce you to the elephant. The Brady commission report states that 60 percent of publicly outstanding common shares are owned by householders. But roughly 80 percent of daily big-board volume is accounted for by institutions such as mutual funds, insurance companies, pension plans, and broker-dealer proprietary accounts. On average, about half of the daily volume on the

72

NYSE consists of block trades, that is, transactions of at least 10,000 shares each. The retail investor, in other words, may own the train, but its operation is firmly in other people's hands. That message was underscored during the October unpleasantness.

The SEC has examined the selling pressure during the critical period, and the results are quite instructive. When the Dow-Jones industrial average fell 95 points on Wednesday, October 14, institutions and broker-dealer trading contributed 74 percent of the sell transactions. On Thursday, with the Dow declining another 57 points, 76 percent of the sales were in those groups. On Friday, with the Dow off what was then a record 108 points, the share was 74 percent again. On Black Monday, the date of the 508-point drop, two-thirds of selling trades belonged to those institutions in broker-dealer accounts.

The retail investors' role pales by comparison. Sales by that group range from 24 percent to 33 percent of total NYSE volume during the key days. Not only did John Q. Public fail to lead the panic in the market, he did not even bother to cash in his mutual fund shares during the period. Redemptions, totaling only 2 percent, were handled easily from available cash reserves.

The retail investor was also the last out of the water. Retail sales in the days immediately preceding Black Monday did not exceed 26 percent of selling volume on the big board, while institutions were selling up to 47 percent, and even the broker-dealer accounts outpaced retail investors by up to 40 percent of NYSE sales. The mix began to change later. On Black Monday retail sales exceeded broker-dealer selling for the first time and inched up to a third of total big-board sales. On October 20, the infamous morning after, the retail investor was finally up a bit, to 37.5 percent of sales, while the percentage of both institutional and broker-dealer selling had declined.

Before we conclude that institutional and broker-dealer trading is not troublesome because so many firms are involved, let me remind you that on Black Monday 14 percent of sales on the NYSE were made by only four sellers. Roughly 20 percent of the selling, amounting to over $4 billion in value and 120 million shares, was done by no more than fifteen sellers. And there were more block trades done on the big board in the five sessions from October 15 through October 21 than in all of 1975.

Finally, the handful of firms that administered so-called portfolio insurance for their clients sold $4 billion of either stocks or futures on October 19. Over the critical four-day trading period from Thursday through the following Tuesday, portfolio insurers would have sold

$20-30 billion in stocks or futures had they been able to carry out their strategy fully.

What all this means is that the securities markets have become highly institutionalized and control of financial assets has become concentrated in a very few hands. A small group of money managers is capable of dictating both the direction and the velocity of equity prices. An important brake on market volatility in past decades, namely, the need for a broad public consensus to develop before a significant change in market trend could occur, has disappeared. From now on, expect sudden twists and turns in the markets as money managers dedicate and withdraw billions of dollars at a time.

Understandably, the various studies of Black Monday do not offer any simple solution to this problem, nor do I have one. Trying to limit the size of funds that specific money managers can control does not seem feasible or even sensible. There may be economies of scale in managing large amounts of money, like lowered transaction costs or better executions, and there is little value in depriving investors of access to top advisers simply because an adviser's money limit has been reached.

Yet a high concentration of investment decision making in only a few hands will necessarily make the markets more volatile, and not just because of the size of the transactions. Chances are those money managers see the bullet coming before the rest of us. They certainly read an ominous message in the market's behavior during the weeks preceding Black Monday while most retail investors suspected nothing. They know how portfolio insurance works and where the trigger points for the sell-off are likely to be. They understand the intricacies of program trading, and they never forget that their performance records are at stake.

Accordingly, at the first sign that their rivals are exiting the market, they feel compelled to follow suit. Although I cannot offer any remedy for this situation, I can suggest that we look realistically at what the markets have become. We should not rely on explanations of Black Monday such as the "loss of public confidence" theory that circulated for a while. These explanations are better suited to a prior era when public investors were allowed to participate in the formation of market trends.

In the meantime, we can do little more than resign ourselves to the fact that with mega-money managers will come mega-market moves. With or without derivative markets, with or without special trading strategies, with or without changes in regulatory jurisdiction, volatility is here to stay, and Black Mondays may no longer be a once-a-generation phenomenon.

74

Thomas Eric Kilcollin

Executive Vice President and Chief Economist
Chicago Mercantile Exchange

One of the recommendations in the Brady report is that there be
unified clearing in the industry. The roots of this recommendation are
fairly obscure. The Brady report refers to several things—large cash
flows that were attendant to the settlement of trades on October 19,
bankers' possible unwillingness to extend credit to their customers,
bankers' having incomplete or fragmented information about positions of customers across various markets, and rumors that certain
clearing entities were not going to be able to fulfill their obligations.
All these concerns got stirred together and out popped a recommendation for unified clearing, on which the the best comment I have seen
was made by Martin Mayer in the *American Banker.* He noted, in
referring to this recommendation, the fine line between meaning well
and meaning nothing at all. The Brady report never really defines
what is meant by unified clearing, but in its extreme form presumably
it would mean that some super clearing agency would clear all stock
transactions, bond transactions, financial futures and options, foreign
exchange, etc. I would like to address whether such an entity makes
any sense.

From a financial point of view, if we were to rank the causes of the
financial problems on Black Monday in rough order of their magnitude, the first one would almost surely be the loss of approximately
$500 billion in wealth. The financial system's weathering of such a
large change in wealth is really quite an achievement. Undoubtedly
the loss put a lot of strain on the system. But it is far from clear that we
would have been better off if that strain had been concentrated in one
clearing entity.

Probably the second biggest cause of problems experienced on
Black Monday arose because of the different contractual features of
the various trading instruments. In the case of stocks, there is a
five-day settlement period; in the case of options and futures, there is
a one-day settlement period. So, for instance, if someone were selling

stocks in order to meet a cash requirement in an option or a futures position, he would have a financing problem because he would not get the proceeds of the stock sale for five days, yet he would have to make settlement on the option or future the next day. This type of gap is really a banking problem, and filling the gap is a banking function. I do not see how unified clearing, or clearing generally, could alleviate this problem.

Another contractual feature is that futures contracts are marked to market with losses paid in cash at least daily. Everyone who loses money must come up with cash, and that cash is passed on to the party that profits. That practice contrasts with both options and securities rules. If, for example, prices fall and an investor has a long put position that he has spread against a long futures position, he will have to come up with cash to meet the loss on the futures positions while his gains in the put position are only accrued. This asymmetry in the timing of cash flows again provides a role for bank financing to fill. No clearing organization will extend credit in such an environment. Doing so is really a banking function.

The banking arrangements of the various clearing members and organizations, and to some extent arrangements within the banking system itself, were the third most important cause of the problems. We experienced bottlenecks and delays, many of which are not surprising in view of the extraordinary volume of funds that had to flow between the institutions. We are working to improve arrangements and to provide better credit facilities. The solution, though, is not unified clearing.

Unified clearing would not have solved the problems of October 19, and it would have introduced at least two new problems. The first one relates to the management of risk. At the Chicago Mercantile Exchange we have a clearing organization, the members of which have unlimited liability for losses. If a firm should default—and one never has—all the other clearing members are immediately liable for the loss. That liability naturally makes people cognizant of what others are doing. Not infrequently, people on our floor call about others who are trading a lot to suggest that they should be checked out. They do that because they have an immediate financial interest at stake. I do not know how a large amorphous organization, where each member has a minor fractional interest, can reproduce this sort of private incentive to monitor risk.

Beyond that, a unified clearing organization would be clearing widely different instruments—stocks, foreign exchange, and, if we include all futures contracts, coffee and sugar right on through to financial futures and options. These are widely disparate commodities, each with its own peculiar risks. It is probably unreasonable to assume that one organization can deal as effectively with all those risks as our current system of multiple clearing organizations. I believe we would lose a measure of our current risk-management ability through a consolidation of the various clearing organizations.

The second problem with unified clearing, perhaps more important than the first, is that it is premised on an old and flawed logic: when you perceive a problem, create a monopoly to fix it. All monopolies sound good on paper, but they seldom work well in practice. There is no reason to suppose that monopoly in clearing will work any better than it does in other enterprises.

In this regard, an interesting recent article in *Barron's* by Mark Weinberg dealt with just this point. Weinberg pointed out a number of innovations in securities clearing that originated from secondary clearing organizations. Continuous net settlement, for example, came from the Pacific Exchange. The Midwest Stock Exchange Clearing Corporation, as another example, branched into clearing Ginnie Maes and also has depository facilities for municipal bonds. These types of innovations and improved service are there because these organizations compete with one another.

We see the same thing in the futures industry. The Chicago Mercantile Exchange, for instance, developed the "mutual offset" with Singapore, and we have improved foreign exchange deliveries to the point that they may be *too* efficient, encouraging delivery through our system rather than through the regular banking system. Each of these innovations has been driven, at least in part, by competitive concerns. Much of this initiative would be lost in a monolithic clearing organization.

Having said all of this, what needs to be done? Principally, we see a need for greater information sharing among clearinghouses. We have had very good information sharing within the futures industry, at least within a subset of the industry. The Chicago Mercantile Exchange, for example, has had an arrangement with the Chicago Board of Trade Clearing Corporation for over five years to share pay and collect information daily on all our joint member firms. We are willing, even anxious, to share that kind of information with every clearing organization. In fact, we have advocated that a group, an intermarket coordinating committee, be created to assess what kind of information various entities need and the best way of making that information available. Such a committee would include the exchanges and the regulators as well as the banks. This is something that can be done that would handle the major problems identified by the Brady commission.

Standardization of procedures could also be expanded. With the Chicago Board of Trade, we have a standardized format for inputting all our trade data. In fact, any firm can submit its trade data to either clearing organization. The data are passed electronically between the clearing organizations. This is an example of the way in which operational efficiency can be improved without resorting to a jointly owned corporation.

Another way is through modifications to the system of intraday settlement variation calls. We would like to routinize these calls so that people expect them and know how to handle them daily. We would also like to standardize them with other exchanges, so that at the time that we are collecting funds on an intraday basis other clearing organizations are releasing funds. Similarly, we would release funds to others when the situation is reversed. We believe there is also merit in looking at cross-margining proposals or at any other proposal that would facilitate financial flows between our clearing organizations.

As Bill Brodsky mentioned, we have taken other steps to increase the financial integrity of our system. These include increased security deposits, a new and improved option-margining system, and a proposed risk-based capital rule.

Roger M. Kubarych

Senior Vice President and Chief Economist
New York Stock Exchange

The analysis in the Katzenbach report is remarkably similar to that presented today by Philip Johnson. The overlap is not 100 percent, but there is certainly a large measure of overlap—to an important extent, this is a market of performance-driven institutional investors who view themselves as small relative to the whole but on any given day are not small relative to the whole market. Those investors say they cannot make much difference to price determination when they transact only $1 billion in a $2 trillion market. But that is an erroneous comparison. Their billion-dollar transactions should be compared with a turnover of trading that is 7 or 8 billion dollars on the average day. This volume makes a big difference at the margin. Even on the biggest trading day in history, October 19, the New York Stock Exchange traded only $21 billion worth of stocks. Something on the order of 5 percent of the total surely has a significant price impact.

As Coffee noted, there are fundamental differences in regulatory philosophy between the securities and futures markets; concepts such as fair and orderly markets, on the one hand, and efficient but volatile markets, on the other. This is a very important point that goes to the heart of the policy debate. There have been some thoughtful pieces written about the difficulties of harmonizing regulatory treatment when there are such great philosophical differences. Part of the struggle over regulatory harmonization has to do with this fundamental distinction.

I do not believe that these philosophical differences can be resolved easily if at all. If they cannot be, we face two questions: How much volatility are we willing to tolerate to get the benefits of efficiency? How orderly do markets have to be to be considered orderly? These are essentially empirical questions that cannot be easily resolved by appeal to some general principle.

On the issue of clearing, the New York Stock Exchange is not involved in the clearing of the trades that take place on the floor of the exchange. That is handled by the National Security Clearing Corporation (NSCC). If a trade takes place between, say, Goldman, Sachs and Merrill Lynch, it goes through a checking procedure and a validation procedure. On the value date a new contract is made with the clearing corporation, and the counterparties change. Credit risk is transferred to the clearing corporation at the point of the clearing.

How does a stock exchange handle the credit risk problem in the meantime, given that the value date is five days in the future? The answer is through the application of surveillance and the net capital rule. As a designated self-regulatory organization, New York Stock Exchange regulatory personnel look at the financial condition of the members of the New York Stock Exchange and assure themselves that firms are in a position to make good on their transactions. The regulatory mechanism in place is essentially a supervisory mechanism. In the area of futures, there is daily marking to market, in large measure because of the cash settlement nature of the instrument.

For the period of October 19 onward, there was no significant issue as to the financial integrity of the NSCC. The recommendations having to do with unified clearing and settlement result from problems that arose in options and futures.

On the issue of trading mechanisms, it is astonishing how little people know about the specialist system. The specialist has a variety of roles that differ enormously with the stock.

Specialists participate, on the average, in only about 12 percent of all transactions. On an average day in the stock market, there are probably 75,000 transactions, with perhaps 8,000 between a broker like Merrill Lynch and a specialist. The other 88 percent take place between brokers.

For a large stock like IBM, which is very heavily traded, specialist participation averages about 1 percent; 99 percent of the time the trade is between two brokers, and frequently it takes place inside the quoted bid-and-offer spread of the specialist.

For large stocks the specialists play the role of auctioneers and agents for limit orders. For small stocks specialist participation, of course, is much larger than 12 percent.

The specialist has an affirmative obligation to participate when one side of the market is empty but a negative obligation not to participate if there is a public bid or a public offer. The specialist has to wait behind the public bid or public offer, according to specified protocols.

Some people have described the specialist as monopolist. I would have to take vigorous exception to that notion. That would imply that there were no other economic agents that provided the same service or product as the specialist. That is simply wrong. The specialist is continuously competing with others, primarily with the block trader, but also with specialists on the regional exchanges. It is not one person who makes a market in, say, IBM stock. All the major trading houses make a market in IBM. They do it all day long. The specialist market in IBM fulfills a unique role within the complex of market-making activities.

There is a mutuality of interest between the big dealers and the specialist. Why? Because the dealers can trade inside the specialist's spread, and they do not have to give up the dealer's "turn." In the over-the-counter market, where there are no specialists, the market makers are generally trading off the end points of their bid-offer spreads. That is simply the economics of the market-making function. By contrast, on the NYSE there is definitely competition in market making for all the big stocks, and the tangible result is effectively narrower spreads.

The specialist system works extremely well under most circum-stances, especially for those stocks where there is a demand for a continuous market—one in which individuals can buy or sell at any moment. The affirmative obligation of the specialist makes possible continuity. Under the kinds of strains of October 19 and 20, the specialist system is going to be stretched well beyond the normal limit.

What did happen on October 19 and 20? It is quite clear, from all the analysis, that the specialists did an admirable job on October 19. It is also quite clear that by October 20 their buying power was signifi-cantly depleted and their ability to "support" the market had dwin-dled. The specialist contribution rose from roughly 12 percent to 18 or 19 percent on those days. The role of the specialist in providing this kind of buffer role continued throughout this period.

But specialists are not central banks. They cannot have a respon-sibility to provide price support one way or another.

Let us turn to the question of trading halts and delayed openings, which can be seen as falling into the category of circuit breakers. These mechanisms have been in effect for a long time and follow from statutory requirements of fair and orderly markets. If the specialist knows that there is a very large order imbalance, it is highly likely that a sharp, discontinuous movement in price may result. Since informa-tion is imperfect, the best thing to do in the presence of large imbal-ances is to announce to everyone the existence of an imbalance and some indication of its size. Obviously, there will still be price changes. But displaying that information gives specialists a far better opportu-nity to find the other side of the trade. That is the basic principle on which trading halts and delayed openings are premised—that they enable information on order imbalances to be publicized and allow the other side the opportunity to come in. The net result is less sharp movements in prices.

Discretionary trading halts have some advantages, the most important of which is accountability. After the fact, one can be second-guessed. Somebody can say, you should not have halted trading. Somebody else can say, you should not have delayed the opening since the order imbalance was not as big as you said. The discipline of accountability engenders a well-considered, well-reasoned decision-making process.

Other kinds of circuit breakers, like price limits, amount to automatic trading halts. Automatic trading halts have other advantages, the most obvious of which is predictability. A greater degree of predictability accompanies, for example, a price list that is known to be imposed under certain stated conditions. Predictability also has considerable value.

I do not think that any of us has the wisdom to decide which is the right type of circuit breaker. With one kind there is an element of discretion and therefore accountability; with the other there is an element of predictability. I am willing to see both sides of that argument. Either way, a strong case can be made for some kind of timeout, as long as it is handled pragmatically. No one wants to go to the extreme of making it impossible for prices to move, since that defeats the whole purpose of markets.

Concern about margin requirements goes to the question of how to secure a level playing field in the stock and futures markets. Lower margins in futures created the misapprehension that there was more liquidity than there turned out to be in a time of stress. People selling futures thought that the futures market was much deeper than it turned out to be. One of the reasons they thought so was that most of the time the futures market depth had been quite strong. One of the main reasons for that was the lower transactions costs, due to the absence of the short-sale rule and the lower effective margin requirements for futures.

There was not a lot of naked short selling on October 19 and 20 as part of the market break. Primarily, people who owned stock thought that they could sell more than they could and found out, after the fact, that although they could sell some stock, they could not sell as much as they wanted as fast as they wanted. In the meantime, prices went down 30 percent.

With a level playing field the relative ratios of cash, stock, bonds, and other financial assets in portfolios would not have become so skewed. Without this illusion of liquidity there would have been less need for a major adjustment in prices. Portfolio managers thought stocks were less risky than they really were, because the convenient and cheap futures market allowed them to build up exposures that after the fact were riskier than they had appreciated.

Appendix

Major Reports on the October 1987 Crash
(in chronological order)

Division of Economic Analysis and Division of Trading and Markets, *Interim Report on Stock Index Futures and Cash Market Activity during October 1987 to the U.S. Commodity Futures Trading Commission,* November 9, 1987 (CFTC interim report).

Katzenbach, Nicholas deB., Esq., *An Overview of Program Trading and Its Impact on Current Market Practices: A Study Commissioned by the New York Stock Exchange,* December 21, 1987 (Katzenbach report).

Miller, Merton H., John D. Hawke, Jr., Burton Malkiel, and Myron Scholes, *Preliminary Report of the Committee of Inquiry Appointed by the Chicago Mercantile Exchange to Examine the Events Surrounding October 19, 1987,* December 22, 1987 (CME report).

Division of Trading and Markets, *Follow-up Report on Financial Oversight of Stock Index Futures Markets during October 1987 to the Commodity Futures Trading Commission,* January 6, 1988 (CFTC follow-up report).

The Presidential Task Force on Market Mechanisms, *Report of the Presidential Task Force on Market Mechanisms,* submitted to the president of the United States, the secretary of the Treasury, and the chairman of the Federal Reserve Board, January 8, 1988 (Brady commission report).

U.S. General Accounting Office, *Financial Markets: Preliminary Observations on the October 1987 Crash* (GAO/GGD–88–38), submitted to congressional requesters, January 26, 1988 (GAO report).

Division of Economic Analysis and Division of Trading and Markets, *Final Report on Stock Index Futures and Cash Market Activity during October 1987 to the U.S. Commodity Futures Trading Commission,* January 29, 1988 (CFTC final report).

Division of Market Regulation, *The October 1987 Market Break: A Report by the Division of Market Regulation, U.S. Securities and Exchange Commission,* February 1988 (SEC study).

85

A NOTE ON THE BOOK

This book was edited by
the publications staff of the
American Enterprise Institute.
The text was set in Palatino,
a typeface designed by Hermann Zapf.
Presstar Printing Corporation, of Silver Spring, Maryland,
set the type, and Kirby Lithographic Company, Inc.,
of Arlington, Virginia, printed and bound the book,
using permanent, acid-free paper.